"*Erik Seversen is the real deal, and his world-traveling lifestyle is inspiring, to say the least. In* Ordinary to Extraordinary, *Erik takes you on an adventure from the first page as he shares his real-life tales of amazing encounters. Through powerful storytelling, Erik demonstrates why we shouldn't be afraid to take chances and why we should embrace the power of moments. Erik is living the life of his dreams, and in* Ordinary to Extraordinary, *he gives the blueprint on how you too can live an extraordinary lifestyle. It's time we follow Erik's lead and stop trying to fit in and do something extraordinary!*"

— JESSE COLE, International Speaker, host of Business Done Differently, and author of *Find Your Yellow Tux*

"*Erik provides numerous stories of adventures he's been on and makes readers reflect with questions at the end of each story. I believe we can change our lives by asking ourselves the right questions, and Erik offers a ton of them. This book gives you the opportunity to learn powerful lessons based on Erik's travels across the globe and helps others go from ordinary to extraordinary.*"

— MARC GUBERTI, Public Speaker, host of Breakthrough Success, and author of *Content Marketing Secrets*

"*From the first page, Erik got me. I was captured by his writing before even knowing what his book was about. He keeps you reading into the night, but Erik's book is more than just entertaining. It transmits an emotional feeling that everything you want to achieve is possible. Ordinary to Extraordinary shows you the many ways we all are extraordinary. This book causes you to reflect on life and meaning. I really enjoyed reading Ordinary to Extraordinary, and I'm sure you will too.*"

— CLAUDIA SCHEFFLER-PERRONE, Owner of Killer Press, Keynote Speaker, Journalist

"I loved this book, as it's not your normal self-help, do this, do that type. These are autobiographical stories of life-changing moments in Erik's life, written like a novel. Characters, storylines, excitement, and even .... don't tell the kids .... naughty stuff. I planned to read this book in one sitting, but upon starting halfway through at "Virginity", I felt drawn to read this chapter multiple times .... go you Erik you bad boy!!! If you are looking for a change in your life and don't know where to turn then this is the place. Seize the moment by buying this book. Then seize every moment in your life from now on .... You will thank Erik as you see your life become the adventure you hoped it would. I'm off to find out where Sabine is now .... anyone seen my French Guide Book?"

— DAVID RALPH, Founder of internationally syndicated
podcast Join Up Dots and Podcasters Mastery Coaching

"Seversen takes the reader on adventure after adventure around the planet! Fellow world-travelers, homebodies, and purpose seekers will be inspired to join the adventure and discover their own transcendental moments, inspired from the true-life tales in this book."

— DEREK CHAMPAGNE, CEO of The Artist Evolution and
bestselling author of *Don't Buy a Duck*

"Erik Seversen is your modern-day adventurer. In Ordinary to Extraordinary, Erik magically transports you to his many adventurous locations. You vicariously experience the world through his eyes and find anticipation in every page. The lingering excitement you feel helps you answer the poignant questions he asks at the end of each chapter to help you create your own daily adventures."

— JAMES MILLER, host of the nationally broadcasted and
syndicated radio show: James Miller | Lifeology

# ORDINARY TO EXTRAORDINARY

# ORDINARY TO EXTRAORDINARY

## STORIES OF EXOTIC PLACES AND REMARKABLE PEOPLE

+

## HOW BELONGING AND PURPOSE CAN TRANSFORM YOUR LIFE

### ERIK SEVERSEN

THIN LEAF PRESS | LOS ANGELES

Library of Congress Cataloging-in-Publication Data
Names: Seversen, Erik, Author

Title: Ordinary to Extraordinary: Stories of Exotic Places and Remarkable People & How Belonging and Purpose Can Transform Your Life

LCCN 2018908868
ISBN 978-1-7323369-1-9 | ISBN 978-1-7323369-0-2 (ebook)
Memoir, Travel Narrative, Self-Development
Cover Design by: Happy Self-Publishing
Interior Design by: Happy Self-Publishing
Edited by: Nancy Pile
Thin Leaf Press
Los Angeles

THIN
LEAF

First things first—thank you for reading this book. I wrote *Ordinary to Extraordinary* to be about you as much as it is about me. If you like what you see and would like to connect with me beyond just the words within these pages, please reach out to me directly. Erik@ErikSeversen.com

If you are the type of person who likes to jump right into things, you should begin the EXTRAORDINARY HABITS CHALLENGE now. This is a list of simple mental and physical habits that, when implemented into your routine, will greatly increase your energy, productivity, and sense of fulfillment. Enact these habits today, so you can find or further develop *extraordinary* success in your life.

You can find the challenge at www.ErikSeversen.com.

To my parents who never tried to stifle the dreams of their children, no matter how ridiculous or impractical.

# CONTENTS

# PREFACE

"The guard at the side of the road was running behind us. *Pop, pop, pop* came the sound of him shooting his rifle in the air. Another guard ran out and threw a spiked board across the road in front of us. We slid to a stop, and three guards in military uniforms and combat boots came running at us—with assault rifles aimed. One of the guards thrust his gun at me and ordered me into a small hut. Then, while viciously yelling that I was a spy, he pointed the machine gun at my face and stuck its end into my mouth. I didn't know what to do. I was paralyzed with fear. I couldn't move. Then he—"

"Wait a minute. You're telling me that a guard in Nigeria put a machine gun in your mouth?"

"Yes," I responded to the guy who had just walked into the conversation from across the room.

"Well, I'm going to call BS," the guy continued, "Somebody over there told me you were telling him that you got bit by piranhas in the jungle in South America."

"That was a different trip," I responded.

"And that's where you lived with an Indian tribe, went on a vision quest, and got malaria?"

"Yes," I confirmed, realizing that I had gotten to the point where the reality of my life started to seem unimaginable to others who didn't know me. You see, for years now, I'd been on a personal quest to find meaning through immersing myself in a variety of experiences all over the world. However, a common reaction when I got talkative at a cocktail party was "Oh my gosh, did that really happen?"

The answer—yes.

The narratives in this collection are an account of actual events from my life. And, indeed, some crazy things occurred, as you'll soon read. Some narratives are about travel, some about falling in love, some about fighting or taking hallucinogenic drugs, and some deal with happy, exhilarating, frightening, or nearly fatal moments that made an impact on me. Plus, I in weave lessons learned, so you, my reader, can more easily benefit from the life experiences shared in this book.

While I wrote this book so you can witness some of my trials and joys without leaving the comfort of your chair, the pages might encourage you to do just that.

Additionally—and perhaps even more so—I wrote this book to compel you to explore your life's meaning. When I write, "life's meaning," I realize it's a big concept. What do I mean by it? I use "life's meaning" to refer to living a life that matters and that's steeped in fulfillment. If, for you, that means seeking out adventures, great. If it means discovering something hidden within your own head or heart, that's also great.

A goal with this book is to immerse you in some of my experiences that have led to my finding fulfillment and living a life that matters in hopes of inspiring you to live with added meaning as well.

In our frantic world where so many of us are trying to juggle too many things at super swift speeds, we find ourselves wondering—*Is this how it is supposed to be? Should we be connected to our jobs or driving our kids to activities 24/7? Are we really supposed to answer that first text as soon as our phone vibrates, even when we're not out of bed yet? Do we know our neighbors? Do we have relationships with people who help us become better? Do we really find joy in work or happiness within ourselves?* While I certainly know individuals who are happy with their lives, I know many others who are wondering, *What is missing?* Or even worse, they are too busy and too preoccupied to even take the time to ask themselves, *What is the meaning of my life?*

Once you take a moment to really ask yourself this question, it is difficult to pretend that the question isn't there. The question, "Does my life have meaning?" will ring loudly at first. However, if pushed aside, it will eventually disappear. Don't let this happen to you. If you can't see the purpose of your life clearly, take action and find your meaning.

To simply find meaning might seem an impossible task, but I have great news for you: it is possible. Emily Esfahani Smith has written a brilliant book, which helps us do just that. In *The Power of Meaning,* Esfahani Smith outlines how anyone can craft a life that matters and find fulfillment in a world misguidedly obsessed with putting happiness, rather than meaning, as a primary goal.

Meaning, according to Esfahani Smith, is made up of four pillars: belonging, purpose, transcendence, and storytelling. By consciously surrounding ourselves with these pillars, we can orchestrate meaning for ourselves. Esfahani Smith writes, "There are sources of meaning all around us, and by tapping into them, we can lead richer and more satisfying lives—and help others do the same."

The book you are reading is about the life of an individual who didn't allow himself to be lulled into a bland existence. Instead, he continually sought to discover meaning. He did this unaware of Esfahani Smith's four pillars, but looking back, he sees that by consciously seeking a life that has included features of belonging, purpose, transcendence, and storytelling, he has created an extraordinary life. One that's been full of adventure, fulfillment, and direction. And, I know, because that person is me.

This book divides my life narrative into unique experiences, each fitting into one of the four pillars. After each section, I show how belonging, purpose, transcendence, and storytelling wove their way into my life, creating a profound sense of satisfaction—all for the sake of challenging, motivating, and guiding you to establish and nurture the four pillars in your life. With the reflective questions at the end of each chapter, you will encounter simple questions to allow you to identify points of meaning in your life.

If you are one of the people who truly enjoys life and is aware of your purpose, I think you will enjoy the adventures of this book. Also, you might become more conscious of the parts of your life that provide meaning to your existence. If you are one of the people who is just going through the motions in life, living day-after-day, doing mostly the same thing, and you are okay, but you're just repeating the mundane, you will find inspiration within these pages. You'll see how by breaking a few of the unwritten rules set by society, you can begin to add a bit of excitement to an otherwise fine existence.

If, however, you are one of the many people who feels that there is something better in life for you, and you are struggling to find what it is, reading this book might provide the very spark that will ignite a wildfire of positive changes in your life. While reading examples of how an average person created a meaningful life and seeing how easy it can be to utilize the power of the pillars to inject meaning into your life, you will be moved to take the small steps needed to build relationships of belonging, decide upon your purpose, and escape the lonely place of ego with a transcendental moment. You might also realize that by telling your story, you can find peace, even if you've had difficulties in your life.

If you are one of the people who is looking for something, the answer is out there, and I know because I was looking too.

# INTRODUCTION

Since I always seemed to be on the move, people often asked me, "What are you looking for?" My most prevalent response was "Nothing." However, now when I reflect, I realize that in fact I was looking for something all along. What I was seeking was the meaning of life—and more specifically, deep meaning in my own life.

As a kid, I always wanted to see what was behind the next corner. If I was riding my bicycle down to the end of the street, I'd always have to peek around the next block before turning around. If I was hiking in the woods at the edge of my neighborhood, I'd always have to peer out beyond the trees to see what was behind them before turning back. As I got older, if I read a stimulating book, I'd also have to read the entire book listed in an interesting footnote. The desire to look just beyond where I was at always existed.

As my world expanded, my looking "around the next corner" took me across the Strait of Gibraltar from Spain to Africa, across seven days of desert to experience Sub-Saharan Africa, and across the Ubangi River to see what was there. It took me behind the Iron Curtain of the Soviet Union and up the Maroni River to live with a remote tribe in South

America. It wasn't only physical places though. Was there meaning in love? I explored relationships. Was there meaning in power? I explored violence. Was there meaning in thought? I explored philosophy. Was there meaning hidden in the depths of the mind? I explored hallucinogenic drugs.

In every case, I was simply following my desire to look around another corner. Eventually while chasing multiple paths of life, I found the answer. As you follow the narratives in this book and see how I came to find the answer to the meaning of life, it is my hope that you are stirred to discover your own answer.

My particular search for meaning took me to many distant lands, and most of the following stories I have related to others, at one time or another, at dinner parties, in cafes, or over a fire pit. I wrote these stories with a tone as if I was simply telling the stories as I've done many times.

Although now I have many stories to tell, my life didn't start out with a compelling desire to travel the world and make relationships with people ranging from hobos to the king of a country. I was born into an ordinary middle-class family in an unassuming suburb of Tacoma, Washington. I was an awkwardly stocky young kid, with a bit of a cowlick, who struggled in elementary school with math and spelling. My major decision for the day was whether I wanted to take the bus at the bottom of the hill or walk the mile or so to school. I felt both lonely and left out at times, but I never allowed my lack of self-confidence stop me from following my dreams, even if they sometimes seemed unreasonable. Ultimately, I ended up with a stack full of extraordinary events in my life.

The narratives in the following collection, however, aren't as much about me as they are about what can happen when an average person decides not to live a normal life. They are about numerous adventures chalked up around the world while meeting interesting people along the way. Looking back, the moments when I went beyond the line of ordinary and entered extraordinary physical and mental spaces are what I like best.

Although I look forward to sharing my adventures, this book is not just about me. I also want it to be about you. At the end of each narrative, you'll find brief questions that are meant to help you reflect on your past, present, and future. Through these, I hope you identify with how easy it can be to construct more fulfillment, meaning, and success in your life simply by being aware of the positivity that already surrounds you and how you can make tiny changes to brighten up the lives of those near you.

# PART 1

# BELONGING

*Compassion lies at the center of the pillar of belonging.*

—Emily Esfahani Smith

# ONE

# ONAWA'S MOTORCYCLE RIDE

*Colorado, USA. 1996. Twenty-Seven Years Old*

Near the end of the day's ride, the wind still felt warm on my face, but I was starting to think of getting some rest. It had been a long ride through Colorado and part of New Mexico. The sun was still up but was getting lower in the sky, and the flashes of blinding sunlight between the tall green trees reminded me that I was riding west on a one-way trip from Virginia to Los Angeles.

Once I hit Chicago, I spent some of my time riding along the original Mother Road, old Route 66. Since I had ridden on the western parts of Route 66 many times, I decided to deviate north a bit to explore the southern parts of the Rocky Mountains.

Gliding around corners and up small hills, I eventually saw a narrow path to the left of the road. Without even thinking much about it, I slowed and turned down the path until it opened into a small meadow of short grass surrounded by tall fir trees.

*Perfect*, I thought to myself. The place was calm and beautiful. I rode a small circle in the field and stopped my Harley facing the small path I had entered from. After I switched the motor off, stillness surrounded me. Putting the kickstand down, I leaned the motorcycle over slowly, making sure the soft ground would hold up the bike. Almost as if I were trying not to disturb the natural scene, I slowly got off the bike, calmly unstrapped my pack from the rear fender, set up camp, and lit a small fire.

Not dark yet, but definitely dusk, I began to think I was hearing things. Small noises were coming from the edges of the clearing. I began to think I was going crazy. *Am I hearing voices?* I thought to myself.

And then she appeared. A very young woman emerged from the woods and slowly walked toward me.

"Are my cousins bothering you?" she asked.

I was still a little shocked, and I stared at her for a moment. She was slightly short and slightly thin. She looked sturdy yet soft at the same time. She had long, perfectly straight black hair.

As she stopped at the edge of my fire, she placed both hands behind her back and repeated, "Are my cousins bothering you?"

"No, not at all," I replied. "I thought I was miles away from anything though."

"You're on an Indian reservation," she explained politely. "We live just over there behind those trees."

"Oh," I said.

She spoke perfect English with an evident Native American accent.

"I think my cousins have been spying on you," she said with a smile. We could hear many kids giggling and running away through the trees.

"Where are we?" I continued.

"On an Indian reservation. We're part of the Apache Nation."

"Oh," I said, "I'm sorry about that. I'll pack my things."

"No, don't," she interjected. "It really isn't a problem. You can stay as long as you like."

"Thank you," I said.

The young woman stood peacefully. She began calmly twisting from side to side, with her hands still clasped behind her back. Her smooth tan face looked serene. She spoke again, "Is that your motorcycle?"

"Yea, I'm crossing the country on it," I replied.

"That would be awesome," she continued, still staring at the machine. "Where are you going?"

"I started in Virginia, and now I'm heading to LA."

"No, I mean which direction," she said.

"West," I answered.

"A lot of my family is west near Four Corners by Mesa Verde," she remarked, "but I've never been there."

"I'll take you," I suggested.

After a few moments discussing it, we agreed that I would take her on my motorcycle to Mesa Verde to meet her relatives the following morning. She was excited, but the calm in her face never left. As if already anticipating the wind, she unconsciously began braiding her long hair, glancing up at me with sparkling brown eyes.

Eventually she sat down across from me. Hours went by, and the two of us, with almost nothing in common, continued to talk and talk. We spoke about her native culture and the modernity of my city. I think we were both secretly jealous of the other. She had never been more than a few miles from the peaceful wooded area where we were sitting, and I had been stuck in traffic jams and crowded cities bustling with people. All she could think about was how exciting it would be to have my lifestyle while I envisioned her calm life removed from the busyness of everything.

It was finally very late and pitch black outside the small ring of light around the fire. The entire evening had been fueled by wood in the fire and curiosity in each of us. At one point, the woman, whom I learned was named Onawa, yawned widely. Then our eyes met, and we laughed at how sleepy each of us had become. In those moments around the fire, we were both in love with each other, but it was a platonic love between two individuals who enjoyed sharing each other's company on a beautiful night in the woods.

Without saying anything, she stood up straight. It was obvious that she was leaving. I stood up as well, and we touched for the first time as we politely hugged each other.

She walked away into the blackness without a light as if she were a blind person knowing every detail of a familiar area.

Although tired, I didn't immediately sleep. It felt like I had just shut my eyes when I opened them again to find the tent lit by the rising sun. I peeked my head out into the bright, crisp morning.

Onawa was sitting peacefully next to the unlit fire near my tent. She looked sad.

"I can't go with you" was the first thing she said.

"Okay, that's fine," I replied as I crawled out of the tent and sat on the grass beside her.

"I'm too scared," she continued. "I don't know how I'll get back."

"No problem. I understand," I responded, a bit sad that she wouldn't be going with me. I dug a small scrap of paper out of my bag and scribbled down the address of the place I was headed to in Los Angeles. "Just in case you ever make it to LA," I said, "here is my address, and you are always welcome to visit."

Onawa took the piece of paper knowing that she'd never make it, but then she got an excited look in her eye. "Hey," she said cheerfully, "can you take me for a ride on your motorcycle to the edge of the reservation?"

"Sure," I agreed.

We both smiled as she helped me roll up my tent and tie my packs to the motorcycle.

"Are you ready?" I asked after she'd climbed on the bike's back seat.

"Definitely," she responded.

I fired up the bike, which sounded like a thunderous roar in contrast to the still, quiet morning.

"Okay, let's go," I announced as I let the clutch out and rode up the path to the main road.

As we turned onto the pavement leaning low to the left, she gripped me tightly and made a small nervous noise, but as we accelerated through the trees, she let out a joyful yell, and I knew that she loved it. I patted the side of her leg and glanced back seeing her long hair trailing in the cool wind. She was smiling wildly.

After only a few miles, she leaned forward, still squeezing me tightly, and put her head on my shoulder for just one brief moment. Then she said sadly, "Here it is."

I saw another small path leading into the woods off to the left. I pulled over and stopped the bike on the side of the road near the narrow opening. We both got off the motorcycle and looked at each other. She still looked exhilarated from the ride. I could tell her heart was beating rapidly.

"Thank you," she said as she leaned in to hug me. I returned the embrace until she relaxed her grip on me, turned, and disappeared into the trees along the path.

It wasn't until I was unpacking my motorcycle after arriving in Los Angeles days later that I noticed an unfamiliar box that was stuffed into the bottom of my pack. It was wrapped in brown paper. I opened it to find a ring. It was a silver ring not unlike others I'd seen down in Navajo country near the Grand Canyon. It was made with blue turquoise and red coral. The silver was in the shape of an eagle on both sides of the wide ring, and the turquoise and coral in the center were in the shape of the Harley-Davidson bar and shield.

*Wow*, I said to myself.

Then I suddenly felt a helpless pit in my stomach knowing that I'd never meet Onawa again. In my mind, I could still see her wide smile and her flowing hair as we shared the brief motorcycle ride. I knew that it was now only a memory, and I'd never get a chance to say thank you to the lovely Apache who lived somewhere in the woods near the border of Colorado and New Mexico.

### *About You*

*Have you ever had a random encounter with a stranger you connected with? Who was it, and how did it make you feel?*

*What could you do to meet an interesting person this week?*

*Do Something Extraordinary*

*Think of someone who has done something that positively affected you, but they might not know it. Say thank you to them.*

# TWO

# ABOVE THE THREE WATERFALLS

*French Guiana, South America. 1995.*
*Twenty-Six Years Old*

I hadn't eaten in two days. There had been a dry spell in successful hunting near the tiny village I was staying in upriver from Pelea on the border of French Guiana and Suriname. This far upriver, I was actually much closer to Brazil than the Atlantic Ocean to the far north. I was over a two-week dugout canoe ride up into the Amazon rainforest.

I had been living in different Amerindian villages for over two months, but this one was by far the most isolated. I was living with the Wayana tribe, but I also encountered Emerillon and a few Yanomamo as well. Downriver from Wayana territory, there was an administrative boundary protecting the indigenous people from entry of outsiders and diseases (I had permission for research). However, it was three small waterfalls that really separated this tiny village from the outside world.

I was excited when Odema, one of the Wayana I had gotten to know quite well, told me that he was going above the waterfalls and that I could come if I wanted.

Traveling as a small group of men in two dugout canoes, we needed a full day to drag the heavy canoes in and out of the water around the falls. Once above them, it was as if the Wayana traveling with me had changed. They became quieter and more serious.

Past the falls, it was still a good distance to the next village. As we were finally nearing it, everyone from that village came down to the edge of the river to greet us. Odema asked me to stay in the canoe while he and the others walked up and spoke with the villagers.

The village consisted of about fifteen people, and absolutely everyone was staring at me. The kids, excitedly pointing, sprinted down to the edge of the water and placed their hands on the tip of the wooden canoe in order to marvel at me.

After a few minutes of speaking with the villagers, Odema walked into the shallow water, grabbed my hand, and led me up to the curious crowd. Odema told me that I was the first non-Indian that some of the people in the village had ever seen. Odema also explained to me that I could hang my hammock in the "public" hut.

Odema and the group had come up to this village to visit relatives, but also for good hunting. But for some reason, no one was successful at getting more than a few fish. Two days later, a few of the men left on a multi-day hunting trip in search of meat farther from the village. The few men remaining were departing for a local hunt earlier than normal, just as I was waking up.

There existed no walls in the huts among the Wayana, so as I slowly opened my eyes in the dark of pre-dawn morning, I could just make out the movement of the men walking quietly out of the village. They carried their bows and arrows parallel to the ground in one hand. These weren't the bows and arrows you might imagine in an old Western film; these were about six feet long and straight with slightly slack strings. Only when the string was pulled back would the bow arch. The arrows were also different. They were about six feet long, and some had magical designs painted on them. Some of the arrow tips were made of bone and were sharp. Some were blunt to knock out small birds. Others were wooden with barbed tips for capturing fish. A few of the Indians had metal-tipped arrows with metal acquired from trading downriver.

I was given a bow and arrow back in Dakoye, where I was living prior to traveling upriver. I also had something many of the Indians didn't—a shotgun with about twenty shells. The discussion about whether I should bring a gun in or not hadn't been a short one. My anthropology professor and I decided that I should bring a gun for two reasons. First, a male who can't provide food would quickly become the village idiot. And second, Brazilian gold miners were starting to come over into French Guiana in search of gold, and they had guns, so it would be better to teach the more remote Wayana about guns from the back side of the gun, rather than them learning about guns from in front of the barrel. Miners were notorious for killing Indians. Earlier when I'd been with a different group of Wayana, I'd seen the seriousness of this firsthand.

In this earlier experience, I was way up the Tampoc River from Dakoye on a multi-day hunting trip. There were three Wayana in the canoe and me. As we were rounding a bend in the river, traveling downstream, I was scanning the trees on the river's right side. Then it was as if someone had pushed a freeze button—the air became instantly tense. I looked to my left and saw a Brazilian gold mining raft. It was about fifteen feet square with hammocks, dirty clothes, and other things hanging along the rafters of its thatched roof.

We were about thirty feet away, just drifting past in our canoe. There were four people on the gold mining raft, and neither they nor any of the Indians was moving.

Also, hanging from the rafters of the illegal mining raft were rifles and revolvers. The Indians I was traveling with had bows and arrows. I had my shotgun, which was lying in the bottom of the canoe near my feet.

Each group stared at the other as our canoe drifted by. I could tell the Indians were petrified. I knew the miners might attack at any moment, and I made the firm decision that I would definitely fire back if it came to it. Thank God it did not.

Finally, when we were out of sight, we talked about what had happened. The Indians were relieved that the miners hadn't tried to kill us.

Rumor about the platform for miners in Brazil was that if there were indigenous people in an area, the miners couldn't mine, but if there weren't Indians, they could. The solution: miners would kill the Amerindians, so they could truthfully say to the authorities that no Indians were in the area.

While I was with the Wayana, I often hunted with my bow. My shotgun served as a backup. As my stomach growled while I climbed out of my hammock, I knew I was on a mission for food. Since I wasn't very good with the bow, I would only take my gun. The problem was that all the adult men had already left, and the jungle could swallow a person who got only a few feet off an established trail. I had hunted with the Indians many times, but I had never gone alone, and the prospect scared me.

So, I decided that I would borrow one of the dugout canoes and check along the banks of the river for crocodiles or iguanas.

As I paddled upstream, I scanned the edges of the river for caiman as well as every inch of the trees for any signs of large iguanas—but nothing. Finally, I decided to get off the river and see if I would have any luck finding wild boar, deer, monkeys, or anything edible.

As I was softly paddling, I noticed a small dirt patch along the steep bank on the right side of the river. I knew it was an animal path. I tied the front of the pirogue to the trunk of a small tree. Balancing as well as I could, I picked up my machete and shotgun, and grabbed a clump of tall grass to help hoist myself up the three-foot, slanted bank. It was obvious animals had used this small path to come to drink, but I didn't see any fresh tracks.

I was only a moment into the forest canopy and away from the incoming light along the river when it seemed to be almost night, even though it was still morning. I gave my eyes time to adjust and then observed intently, looking for unique trees, so I could later recognize where I had entered the jungle. I knew that a short span of non-attention could mean that I'd be lost, and I mean—really lost. Being lost in unfamiliar territory was common, even for the Indians. It had happened to a teenage Wayana and me a few weeks earlier. It took us almost a full day to find our way back, and I wouldn't have been able to do it alone.

Once I was confident I could recognize at least this spot, I began walking slowly. I felt a serene quietness fill me. I walked softly, and I could barely hear my own steps. The animal path was actually well trodden with a few tricky sidetracks. I was marking trees with my machete showing where I had come from, so I was feeling pretty good.

My thoughts were focused, but as time went on, I had to fight to keep my mind from drifting. At one point, I had to fight the theme song from Jeopardy out of my head.

A meal could be anywhere: in the trees, on the jungle floor, right behind me. As more time passed, I started to feel my hunger. I had paddled for over an hour, and now I estimated that I had been walking for over three. I knew I had to turn around soon, but I felt like I would find something in just a few more yards, just a few more yards.

Finally, I heard something—the first sound I'd heard in a long time. I looked up to see two macaws high above me. Once they saw me, they started croaking loudly. That wouldn't be good for me to surprise anything. I thought about shooting them and eating them, but quickly forced the thought out of my mind. I'd eaten a few toucans with the Wayana, but never the majestic bright red, blue, and yellow macaws.

I decided that I should turn around.

Terror struck me. I had only stopped for a few minutes and had taken only a few steps in different directions to get a better view of the birds mocking me from high above, but when I turned around, the trail was gone. While walking along it, I was sure I was following an easily recognizable trail, but it was nowhere to be found. My heart rate immediately doubled. I stood absolutely still, so I wouldn't disturb any of the precious marks on the jungle floor that could serve as clues to where I had come from.

I finally made a note of a few particular trees about ten feet on either side of me, and I did the same to two more trees, making a square area where I guessed I might have come from. I wasn't entirely sure which direction even that was. Being near the equator, the sun didn't really help for north or south unless near the beginning or end of the day for east/west, so I randomly named one of the sets of trees north, and I walked back and forth between all the trees. Since I was moving slowly, walking back and forth between the trees seemed to take forever. I began to panic, which was the worst thing to do.

I walked back and forth about five times before I finally saw the now tiny path. A wave of relief filled me.

It took a bit of time for me to gain my composure, and the fright had expended a lot of my energy, but at least I knew which way to go. I rested for a moment and drank some fresh rainwater trapped between a large jungle palm frond and its tree trunk.

At first, I was happy just to be back on the path again, but then the desperation for food crept back into my thoughts. I started praying. "Please, dear Lord, let me see a pig," I'd say. Then I'd repeat, "Please, dear Lord, let me see an agouti." Then, "Please, dear Lord, let me see a deer. Please, dear Lord, let me see a bush turkey," and "Please, dear Lord, let me see a monkey." And I did.

I first heard the rustling of the leaves. I looked up. A very large, black spider monkey was above and in front of me, but he was at least a hundred feet up in the trees. I stopped. I tried not even to breathe. The monkey was still too far away for a shot. I crept slowly, watching the back of the monkey as he was busy chewing on something. I crept as quietly as possible. My heart rate increased. Strangely, I didn't even think of just the meat I'd be able to eat if I got the monkey, but I imagined the celebration in the village as I returned with a large monkey. I'd parade around the center of the village, and they would all think I was a hero. An adult spider monkey is delicious and could feed everyone in the village.

I forced the celebration out of my head. My pleading prayers changed to "Please, dear Lord, let me get this monkey. Please, dear Lord, let me get this monkey." I kept repeating this. The monkey seemed larger and larger the closer I got to it. I became anxious. My focus was intense, and I was just about in comfortable range. The monkey wasn't too far away, but he was high in the trees.

I knew I needed to get about twenty feet closer for a good shot. I slowly raised the barrel of my shotgun in the direction of the monkey and calmly placed the gun's butt against my shoulder. I was aiming right at the animal, but I needed a few more yards.

I was just about there when the monkey jerked. He was sitting between two branches with leaves all around him. He looked in my direction, made an ungodly noise, and jumped.

I pulled the trigger—and an explosion of sound filled the woods—but he was gone. As he jumped from tree to tree, there was no pretending I would catch up to him. I couldn't leave the trail to follow him.

I became depressed. I imagined not the joy of the villagers when I returned with meat, but the silence as they watched me return from another day hunting with nothing. I was mad at God, and I even started negotiating with God that if he allowed me to find some food on the way back, I'd be perfect forever. It didn't work. In fact, I think God didn't like this negotiating based on what would happen later that day.

As I continued back the same way I had come, my mind went back and forth from the Jeopardy theme song to being very focused. In the hours I was in the forest on the way back, I saw nothing other than one small boa constrictor.

It was afternoon when I got to the familiar opening where the pirogue was tied. I stood at the top of the bank for a moment, negotiating how I would get down into the boat. First, I very carefully tossed my machete into the bottom of the small boat, all the while holding my shotgun in my left hand. Next, rather than grabbing the grass as I had done to ascend, with my right hand I grabbed a thin vine-like tree trunk, which allowed me to slide down the leaf-covered muddy bank.

I was awkwardly dangling from the vine-like tree trunk and almost sitting on the canoe bench when I felt it.

The sting was profound. It was on the tip of my right elbow. The boat was wobbling, and I fought for balance. My left hand was still occupied with the gun, and I still couldn't let go of the vine without falling into the water, unless I got more of my weight over the center of the canoe, but it didn't matter. It had already happened. The small rust-colored scorpion was up-righting itself as it scurried back under the leaves along the bank. I let myself awkwardly slide into the boat.

The pain felt like a serious bee sting. I could handle the pain, but my heart raced as I wondered how bad the sting would become and what kind of scorpion had stung me. In Africa, a few years earlier, I had heard that small scorpions were worse than large ones, but I really didn't know. I began to panic. I tried to remain calm, knowing that for snake bites, keeping the heart rate down was important, so the poison wouldn't move around the body as quickly. I assumed it would be the same. There was a battle in my head between the desperate prayers I was whispering and the echo of *Oh shit* that kept creeping into my mind.

It was hard for me to even see the tip of my elbow. After I pulled the skin around, I could see a bright red dot. Not educated in treating scorpion stings, I just squeezed the area with my left-hand thumb and index finger, but I didn't know if it did anything or not. As quickly as I could, I untied the front of the canoe and let the current pull the nose of the canoe around, facing the direction of the village.

At first, I was paddling normally, but I wanted to keep my heart rate down, and my right arm began to burn worse and worse, so I stopped. I squeezed the area again, but I could tell that this was doing nothing to push any of the poison out. I kept praying. Also, I was happy that I was upriver from the village.

As the pain increased in my right arm, I ended up just holding it against my body. I used my left had to hold the paddle as a rudder. While I was floating along, the pain was spreading. It felt like poison was traveling up the veins in my arm and down into the right side of my chest. By the time I reached the village, my entire right arm was numb and useless.

As the front of the pirogue slid up against the shore, I was pleased that there was a small sandy beach in the bend of the river right in front of the village. I stepped into the shallow water and pulled the canoe up onto the beach. Other than a few women, the village was empty, so I just walked over to my hammock and, with great difficulty, got in.

I didn't know exactly how long I was in my hammock before Odema came over, carrying my shotgun and machete. He casually placed the gun in the hut's rafters and said that they'd had a successful hunt and had gotten a pig. I was already vaguely aware of this because I had heard villagers cheering when the hunting party returned.

While that was great news, I had other things on my mind. Because Odema spoke a bit of French, I desperately uttered, "*Je suis très malade,*" or "I'm very sick."

I was sweating profusely. Odema looked at me with a horribly concerned face but didn't say anything.

"*J'ai été piqué par un scorpion,*" I continued. I tried to move my right arm up to show him, but it didn't move, so I rolled over, with great pain throughout the whole right side of my body. My left hand was mostly stuck between my body and the hammock, but I tried to point at the mark on my elbow.

Odema crouched to examine my elbow. He poked my arm a few times near the elbow and then near my shoulder. The worry in his face worsened. He began mumbling to himself. He put his hand on my forehead, just as a concerned mother would do to a sick child checking for fever. Still without saying anything, he left. He soon returned with water, which I drank with his help. Then he told me to rest.

Later that night, Odema checked on me again, gave me more water, and then crawled into his own hammock, which hung next to mine. I didn't have a hard time falling asleep, but I woke up many times shivering. I got through the night in a dream-like state of being asleep and awake.

In the morning, everyone was up at first light. Odema again checked on me and gave me water. We still hadn't said more than a few words about anything. I didn't mind because each word made my head and body ache. I could barely remember the limited French I knew anyway. I was becoming delirious.

Odema brought me a few fatty scraps of the boar that had been cooked the night before. Although it was miserable to eat, I forced down the much-needed food. Most of the village was now at my side, and all looked concerned. They had saved some of the softest and best parts of the meat for me, which I greatly appreciated.

After eating, Odema was gone for a while. I just lay there, stuck in the hammock, with the right side of my body absolutely paralyzed. My breath was becoming faint, and it felt like my chest was also numb. The Indians from the village never left me. There were at least a few who sat near me concerned the entire time.

When Odema came back, he wasn't alone. He was with a shaman. The shaman was dressed the same as all the other men with a string cord holding up a short red cloth hanging from his waist and nothing else. However, he also had geometric designs painted on his arms and chest. He stood over me, intensely examining my whole body. He put his hand on my chest for about a minute. I looked up at him. I couldn't even smile. I felt faint and just lay there, conscious that at least my eyes were open.

Next the shaman sat on a small stool. He picked up a fist-sized yellowish-brown gourd that he had brought. He poured a bit of water into the gourd and then very deliberately dropped a small, round pebble into it. His eyes went into a distant stare vaguely in my direction, and he placed the gourd just below his mouth near his chin as if it were a microphone. He began chanting.

I didn't know what he was saying, but the pattern was *na, na, na … na, na, … na*. The first three syllables were low notes, the middle two were a bit higher, and the last was much higher than the others with an upward swing at the end. Then he would repeat. Over and over the shaman did this for hours and hours. He was rocking slowly for most of this, and he didn't seem to pause once during the entire time. His stare was entirely fixed. Finally, he stopped, stood, put his hand on my chest again, and then slowly walked away.

I lay in the hammock for three days. I could literally feel the poison in the right half of my body, but it was the fever and chills that made me delirious. I never really thought to myself that I would die right there, but at times in my delusional agony, I actually wished for it. I knew that my body was seriously going in that direction. It was one of two times in my life that I spoke in prayers with God accepting the idea that I really might meet Him soon.

The shaman returned each day and did the same chanting for about four hours each time. The villagers had me drinking bark tea and encouraged me to chew on bark from a tree.

I learned later that the shaman only performed that particular ritual when he thought someone was going to die. I also didn't learn until later that at the same time I suffered from the scorpion sting, I was also in the advanced stages of malaria. After hundreds of mosquito bites, malaria had been dormant in my system. The shock to my body from the scorpion sting then activated it. The bark the Wayana were giving me contained quinine, similar to the medicine I had taken back in the USA after my first malaria attack from when I was in Africa.

Even when the effect of the scorpion sting subsided, my fever due to malaria continued. It was obvious that I had to get downriver and out of the forest. I had planned on being in the jungle for anthropology research for three months, and the end was coming soon anyway. Odema was planning on staying in the isolated village for a few more weeks, so he couldn't take me out, but he helped me arrange passage downriver.

One of the oldest men in the village volunteered to paddle me down as far as Antecume Pate, a Wayana village on the Suriname side of the river a few days away. From there, I could easily get another canoe to Maripasoula, a rural outpost of about a thousand people that had a French doctor whom I was anxious to see. The cost for the man's volunteering to paddle me out was my shotgun and the remaining twenty shells I had left. It was an easy choice.

In the dugout canoe, we made a pile of palm fronds, so I could recline in the bottom of the boat rather than sit on one of the benches. Even still I was up and walking around by the time I left the village, a necessary condition since I would need to help the old man slide the canoe around the falls on the way out.

Saying goodbye to the people in this small, isolated village was tough. I would have loved to stay with them longer, but that wasn't possible. It was hard to say goodbye to Odema, but it was the shaman that was most difficult. I could say, "*Ipoc moni*," which translates as "Thank you" in Wayana, but staring deeply into his eyes as I held his hands in front of me was the only thing I could do to try to express how much I appreciated his efforts while my body had been dying. The shaman was one of the oldest in the village. Tears beaded in both of our eyes as he gave me a mostly toothless grin. All the villagers were amazingly sympathetic towards me, but I somehow felt like the shaman had actually experienced the pain and anxiety with me.

My chauffeur pushed us into the current and jumped into the back of the canoe proudly carrying his new shotgun. I waved goodbye to the people who had cared for me.

## *About You*

*Have you ever become close with a group of people in a short amount of time? What was the situation and what allowed you to become close with them?*

*Generally, do people help others who are in need? Why or why not?*

*Imagine that you just survived a near-death experience where strangers helped you get through it. What would you say to them?*

*Do Something Extraordinary*

*If you survived an ordeal getting a "second chance" on life, is there anything you would change in your life? Make that change now.*

# THREE

# THE BERBER'S SONG

*Morocco, Africa. 1989. Twenty Years Old*

I was in Morocco. I enjoyed the camels on the beaches of Tangier, the modern sights of Casablanca, and the bustling markets with spices and snake charmers in Marrakesh.

To see something different, I decided to get way off the beaten path. I pulled out my worn map and selected an area about one hundred kilometers wide, lying between tiny roads. It was basically a blank area of the map, showing nothing at all. I decided to see what was or wasn't there. I packed my huge canvas backpack with eight loaves of bread, a few cans of meat, and fourteen liters of water, and I headed out into the sand.

During the first few miles, I felt like I was getting nowhere, but as I kept up my slow pace, allowing myself to stop and rest only about every hour, I began to make some progress. It was hot, and when I say hot, I mean triple digits hot. I realized that I definitely should not have left as late in the morning as I had. I wouldn't make that mistake again.

From bottom to top, I wore Birkenstock sandals, khaki pants, a loose-fitting white three-quarter sleeve shirt that I had gotten in Marrakesh, and a white turban wrapped around my head and face. Of course, I also wore the very heavy backpack, which pushed my posture to a slightly forward hunch as I walked.

The going wasn't easy, but I hadn't expected it to be. It was near the end of the day, and the temperature was beginning to decrease a bit. It wasn't time for me to take my normal break, but I wanted to check my compass to make sure I was still heading due east as was my plan.

I wasn't following any trails. I didn't know of any to follow. The terrain wasn't totally flat; it was composed of sand, gravel, and a few rocks and shrubs. I struggled to focus on the compass due to salty sweat pouring into my eyes. I wiped the stinging sweat with the end of my turban. I blinked a few times, and then, as if by magic, I saw a person standing about twenty feet away.

The person had very dark skin, and he was wearing a gray turban and a long white tunic. We seemed equally shocked to see each other. We stared at each other for a moment. Then the man smiled broadly and waved at me excitedly. He walked over and began speaking to me in a language I didn't understand. He grabbed my hand and began pumping it up and down in an extremely excited handshake. He just kept talking, smiling, and shaking my hand. I smiled in return, and he grabbed my hand with both of his. He politely began pulling me as he started to walk north.

I didn't know exactly what to do, but I immediately felt safe with this young man who must have been about sixteen years old. Eventually he let go of me with one of his hands but continued to hold my hand as we walked. After about ten minutes, we came upon a worn footpath. When we rounded a hill, I was suddenly confronted with an orchard of fig trees. The path widened, and I could see other plants and trees in the oasis. A few kids gathering figs saw us and ran over excitedly, and then two other men came over. All were very excited, and we became a small parade as we walked into a very small village of brown adobe houses. We passed a few donkeys, and the guy who was holding my hand led me right through the village to a small rectangular building.

As we entered, I could see that it was a makeshift schoolroom. There was another young man erasing the chalkboard. He turned, and the teenager who brought me there evidently told the teacher that he had found someone in the desert. I wish I could have understood exactly what he was saying because it must have been comical.

The teacher smiled as widely as all the others who were crowded around me, and he spoke to me in French. I could tell that he was asking where I had come from, and I attempted to reply in French. Then he asked if I spoke English. I replied, "Yes," and the conversation switched to his bad English, which was much better than my bad French. The first thing he said to me was that Mohammed, the guy who had found me, asked if I would have tea at his family's home.

"Sure," I agreed, looking at Mohammed, who was still smiling widely.

As a group, we walked over to Mohammed's house, which was one section of a larger adobe structure with two levels and multiple living quarters. From all corners of the small village, veiled women and men in turbans stared. We stopped at the entrance of the house, and two kids ran in and returned with two adults and an extremely elderly woman who was obviously the grandmother of the home.

I shook hands with the man, as the teacher, who was named Abdul, introduced us. Then we entered the low dark entrance, circled up cramped adobe stairs, and entered a room with two open doors and two small window openings. There was a small cooking fire burning in the middle of the room, and I was served very strong hot mint tea and sugar in a small glass. I could tell Mohammed's mother, who was wearing a black burka, was trying not to stare at the new stranger in her home.

Almost everyone from outside had come into the room with us, but only the adults were served tea. With the help of the schoolteacher, we began talking. They learned about how I simply wanted to walk through a remote part on the map. I learned that they were a Berber tribe that had lived in the village for generations. They said many times how lucky they were that I had found their village, but I was the one who felt lucky. Although only about forty miles from the nearest village, they said they didn't get any visitors from the outside.

As soon as the first tea was finished, I was asked to have tea at another household, and then another. I had only been in the village for about two hours when I'd been given tea in four homes. As it was getting late, the teacher translated for Mohammed who asked if I would stay the night at his family's home. I enthusiastically welcomed the idea, especially as it meant I wouldn't have to set up my tent.

The entire family of six people and I slept on the floor in the same large room. I slept very well drifting to sleep in awe of the amazing situation I had found myself in. As I relaxed into sleep, I was aware of the light smell of smoke from the cooking fire, the large colorful rugs that carpeted the dirt floor, the multiple glasses of mint tea, and the many warm smiles from all the lovely people in the village.

The next day, I explored the garden and orchard with Mohammed and all the other youth in the village. I was asked to teach the kids some English words in the schoolroom. I was asked to drink tea with pretty much every adult we passed. I welcomed the first of the many glasses of the sugary tea. But my politeness by not refusing the offers caught up with me as I felt like I was getting an overdose of sugar. Finally, I had to start refusing because my skin was getting a rash from so much sugar. They began offering me warm sheep's milk instead.

The evening of my first full day with the Berbers was to be kind of a feast in my honor. We stepped into the "chicken coop," which was basically a large roofless open area on the second floor of the adobe compound. Mohammed's family only had two chickens, and they wanted to give one to me. We all went out together to get the chicken. As a sign of respect, Mohammed's dad caught it and handed it to me. I stood there holding the chicken wondering why everyone was staring at me. Mohammed, who was now speaking a bit of the French he had learned in school, told me that I should kill it.

"Oh," I said, and I asked him to show me how they did it. We laid the chicken on the ground and placed a small wooden board underneath the chicken's neck. Mohammed showed me that we had to grab and pull the chicken's tongue out a bit, face it in a certain direction, extend the neck long, and slice quickly the chicken's neck. I did all these things. Everyone looked proud of me until I let go of the chicken too soon and although totally dead, it began to run around wildly, creating a frantic ruckus of feathers and dust. I chased it for a moment. One of the kids tossed a wicker basket over it to stop the flapping bird. The meal was splendid.

What wasn't splendid is what happened later. The next day, I had to go to the bathroom. Since we were in the desert miles from the nearest store, toilet paper wasn't an option. Going number one was easy, but for number two, I'd have to tell someone that I needed to go, and they would tell Mohammed's mom who would warm up a cup of water over the fire. The toilet was in the center of the chicken coop. It was made up of a flat board over a small slit in the ground, which led to the pile of manure in the room below.

I had done this a few times, but on this day, things went horribly wrong. First, I mentioned that I had to go, and Mohammed's mom warmed up the water and handed the cup to me. I went into the chicken coop, squatted down, and did my business. All good so far, but oops … I missed the small opening in the dirt floor. *No problem*, I thought, *I'm going to wipe with my hand anyway, so I can just push the pile into the hole and clean up with the water.* As I spun around to do the deed, I had just moved the mess with my fingers, when my foot bumped into and tipped over the precious cup of water.

*Oh no*, I said to myself as my stomach sank. *Oh no*, I said again as I began to panic. I couldn't walk back into the room with crap all over my hand. In desperation, I just rubbed my hand and fingers in the small pool of mud as best as I could, but it really didn't help.

Horribly embarrassed, I walked back into the room with Mohammed's family. No one said anything, but the smell was undeniable.

I waited as long as I could, which was about ninety seconds. Then I said I needed to go again.

As if relieved, Mohammed's mom started warming up the water, but in desperation, I gestured that it was fine— no need to warm up the water for this one. I went back up and washed much better this time.

The meals were also culturally very different to what I was accustomed. Basically, all the adult men in the village, which were about eight, and I would sit in a circle on a large rug usually outside. One of the women would bring bread and another would bring a very large dish full of food, which was always couscous or rice. She would set it in the middle, and we'd eat from the common dish with our hands carefully avoiding the "dirty" left hand.

Every evening as we ate the meal, there would be one special piece of meat, usually a single chicken leg or the like, sitting in the center of the large bowl atop the grains. At the end of the meal, as the dish was getting near empty, the piece of meat would remain. The men would look at me proudly, indicating that it was for me.

About halfway through one of the meals, I realized that the day's piece looked a bit odd. We were eating small strips of goat, and I realized that it might be a goat's testicle. Of course, at the end of the meal, there was only one thing left, and as always, the men proudly looked up and smiled that this prize was for me.

I picked the testicle up, and as I was bringing it to my mouth, I didn't know whether I should bite into it or put the whole thing in my mouth at once. In my haste, I chose the latter. This was definitely the wrong decision. The ball of meat in my mouth was so large and slippery that I was having a hard time getting my teeth around it. It was starting to gag me, partially because of the thought of what I was eating, but mostly because it was so large and round. I began to panic as to where I'd vomit if it came to that. Would I turn and hope to miss the rug? Should I aim for the dish we had just eaten from?

As I struggled, all the men's eyes were on me. I got the feeling that they didn't know what to do either. I could tell they wanted to help somehow, but what could they do? It was a horrible moment. I even began to sweat.

In the end, I got it down without vomiting. After I finally swallowed the last bit and smiled, they all started cracking up. The proper and polite tone of our dinner together finally went out the window, and we all laughed until tears rolled down our faces.

At the end of every day, we would all agree that I would be leaving early the following morning. Then every morning, it was decided by the villagers that it was too late and too hot for me to leave, so I'd have to stay another day. Then the day I actually did get up very early, they said that it was to be the Prophet Mohammed's birthday the following day, so I had to stay for the celebration.

The festivities surrounding Mohammed's birthday mainly revolved around sitting and eating and drinking tea all day. It was great to spend the last day with the whole village together.

The following morning, I woke up just as it was getting light. I packed up my sleeping bag and backpack as Mohammed's mom and grandmother were preparing the day's breakfast.

During the four days I was in the Berber village, there was certainly a respectful shyness, and the closest that I had come to touching any of the women was accepting a cup of tea or a snack of corn or figs from one of them. However, at my departure Mohammed gestured that I should hug his grandmother goodbye. She had done so much for me, and he obviously mentioned it to her as well. Laughing and feigning bashfulness at the start, the elderly woman finally embraced me and pressed her veiled face against my cheek. The village erupted in applause. It was as if I was an excuse to break the rules a little bit in a very innocent way with the lovely old matriarch of the village.

After the emotional hug, Mohammed's grandmother waved to me as I began to walk away, and everyone began walking with Mohammed and me. It was about a quarter mile or so to the remote cement whitewashed gate that marked the edge of the village. There was no fence, just an enormous gate with sand surrounding it on all sides. The gate was on a small hill, and when we got there, I shook hands with all the women, and I hugged all the men. Mohammed and I had spent almost every minute of four days together, and it was very sad to say goodbye to him, but it was time to move on.

As I began walking down the small slope along a path that would lead me to Alnif about forty miles away, my pack felt heavy, but I trudged forward. That's when I heard a few of the women begin singing a beautiful song. It was a lovely and peaceful song, and it filled me with love for the villagers. As I kept walking, the children joined in the singing. Many, many minutes later, I could tell that the entire village was still singing in my direction.

When I looked back, I could see the image of the villagers standing at the crest of the hill. I waved widely, and I smiled knowing that they could no longer see my face. I looked down at the bright white tunic I was wearing, which they had given me to wear for Mohammed's birthday celebration. I wanted to run back and hug everyone again, but I was much too far away for that. I turned and plodded on, and the singing continued but became more and more faint as I walked.

At one point, I didn't know if I could hear them or not, so I turned to see the dotted specs still at the top of the distant hill. I knew that they were still there singing. Eventually the singing faded and then returned and then faded again, finally yielding to the still silence of the desert.

Hours after I had left the village and was just getting into the extreme fatigue from the exertion of walking and the exposure in the sun, I heard the Berber singing right behind me. I dropped my pack and spun around, but there was nothing. I could still hear the music though. It wasn't faint or abstract but crystal clear. It was like a mirage for my ears. I could even hear the individual voices of the singers whom I had spent the prior four days with. I could picture their individual faces. They were with me.

Immediately I felt emotional because of that special gift of song they had given to me. I was convinced that the Berber tribe knew that their song would return to my ears as I pushed forward fatigued under the sun. They knew that it would encourage me, and they knew that I would be affected by their care, their hospitality, their friendship, and their love toward the random twenty-year-old from across the world who stumbled into their tiny village in the middle of the Moroccan desert. They knew that with their song I would never feel alone in the desert.

## About You

*Have you ever been overwhelmed by someone's generous hospitality? Where was it, and how did it make you feel?*

*What are some simple things anyone can do to make someone feel welcomed and loved?*

Do Something Extraordinary

*Invite someone into your home, maybe a random traveler or a friend for dinner, and make them feel like a royal guest. Plan what you can do to make them feel extra special.*

# FOUR

## GOURMET DUCK

*Virginia, USA. 1995. Twenty-Five Years Old*

"Where'd you get the duck?" Edy asked over our candlelit dinner on the small, square wooden table in her living room. The lights were low. It was a beautiful setting with an amazing meal of roast duck that Edy had prepared.

Edy, a sassy Puerto Rican from New York with reddish hair and big green eyes, was one of my friends. We were both grad students at the University of Virginia.

She delicately placed another bite in her mouth. She smiled at me, looking wonderful, and waited for me to answer her question.

"In Alabama," I answered.

"Did you go hunting?" she continued.

I really didn't want to tell her, but she'd learn in the end anyway.

It all started a few days earlier when I was driving to the university library to study, and I wasn't entirely happy about it. Tareq, one of my best friends, had had plans to come over from LA to visit me in Charlottesville. We would catch up over a four-day weekend. I was a grad student at the University of Virginia, and he was doing his PhD at UCLA. For a few weeks I had been looking forward to seeing him.

"Erik, I've got bad news," Tareq said on Friday evening, the day before he was supposed to arrive. "Something has come up, and I can't get out of it." I knew he would have made it if he could have, but it didn't make me any less bummed.

About halfway to the library, feeling a little down, the song "Sweet Home Alabama" sounded on the radio of my old red Chevrolet with a Harley-Davidson sticker in the back window. I turned it up and felt better already. Then I got really excited. I turned the car around and went back to my place, picked up my cowboy hat and a bottle of Jack Daniels, and began to head south … toward Alabama. I decided that studying that weekend wasn't going to be in the cards, so I would make an adventure. I had a credit card on me, but I decided not to use it. I would spend only the small amount of cash I had in my pocket. I didn't know exactly how much I had, but I knew it wasn't much for a trip, but I felt free.

Heading south on Highway 29, I was already having fun. After a few swigs from the bottle, I was going about 90 miles per hour in my overheated car when I passed an old biker on a beautiful 1950's two-tone, blue and cream Panhead. In my eagerness to check out the bike, I slammed on the brakes weaving all over my lane before gawking at one of the coolest old bikes I'd seen in a long time. After a good look, I hit the accelerator again and continued on until a few miles later, I saw a biker bar in Lynchburg. Without a thought, I pulled in, got out, and headed for the door to grab a beer.

It turned out that although there were many bikes out front, it actually wasn't a bar, but an old Harley shop, so I went in and mulled around, looking at various parts and dreaming of what I could do to modify my Sportster, which was sitting at Old & New Customs motorcycle shop waiting for repairs. As I began to walk out the front door, I was confronted by a big burly 250-pound biker with a beard down to his large belly.

"You!" he hollered as we almost bumped into each other. He then pointed at me and declared, "You almost killed me …"

"Sorry, man," I replied. "I got excited when I saw your beautiful bike."

He, being decades older than me, seemed almost amused, but he still gruffly pushed past me and entered the shop. I stood in front of the glass panel window and began talking with a few locals.

A bit later, the bear I'd almost hit came out. He walked right up to me and casually tossed me a t-shirt, muttering, "Least you have good taste, kid. Here's a little souvenir for you."

I caught the shirt and spread it to see the wide wings of a soaring eagle with the scripted words "Harley-Davidson" on the top and "Lynchburg, Virginia" on the bottom.

"You're kidding me," I said. "Thank you very much."

He obviously knew I wasn't from around these parts. He smiled and said, "A little memory of your trip." As he got on his bike, he primed the kicker, hopped up with all his weight on the kick-starter, and the bike fired up loudly with him rolling away in a cloud of dirt.

In the late evening, I rolled into Nashville. Just because of the allure of the name Nashville, entering the city made me excited. I even splurged a bit with my money sipping beer until after midnight while listening to some of the best country music in the world. There is always something special about live music in a bar, and in Nashville it felt even more magical as I tapped my boots letting the culture of the place fill me.

I knew that I didn't have enough dough for a room, so I continued south until at about three in the morning, feeling a bit tired, I pulled to the side of the road to pick up a hitchhiker. I assumed he'd walk up to the car, but after about ninety seconds, I finally looked back to find out that it wasn't a hitchhiker after all—it was a small tree. Realizing that I was probably way more tired than I knew, I pulled my seat back and slept right there.

The next morning, I woke up fresh to the sound of passing cars and continued down to Birmingham and on to Montgomery and Mobile. Inspired by the great Lynyrd Skynyrd, I'd made it to Alabama.

It was certainly a beautiful place, but in Montgomery, I was reminded that not all evils of the Deep South had been exorcised. I wanted to get a glimpse of the Civil Rights Movement and was told that there was some sort of museum somewhere. I never found it. Maybe there was one somewhere, but I wasn't able to locate it. I knew that I should have been close based on the directions I had been given. I was in a rundown neighborhood, and I asked as many people as I could where it was, but the responses from both white and black people I asked were the nature of "Why would you want to go there?" and someone even said this directly.

I was sure there were some great things in Montgomery, but I certainly didn't feel welcome. In my black cowboy hat, Harley shirt, dirty jeans, and old cowboy boots, most of my interactions were brief. In this town and on this day, I felt my look represented a stereotype of acceptance of intolerance and maybe even direct bigotry, and this disturbed me.

At one point I was walking toward a skinny black man wearing an old baseball cap. As I looked toward him to ask directions, he paced a few feet further away from my path. With his hand, he turned his cap at an angle, so I wouldn't see his face. This man was obviously terrified to have any interaction with me. In this case, I think it was simply because of my look as well as that I was white, so I let it go, found my car, and continued on my way, feeling a somber emotion as I left.

Realizing that my money was almost gone, I calculated how much I would need for gas to get back to Virginia and looked at even less remaining. I was now getting hungry, and it was getting late. I was looking for a place to camp when I decided that I didn't have enough money for dinner. There really wasn't any place around to eat at anyway.

I was in the woods heading toward Georgia when I saw it—a dead squirrel in the middle of the road. *Dinner,* I thought. I pulled over and walked up to the squirrel. I poked it with my finger, happily finding it very soft, almost warm. I knew it hadn't been there for long, and it was only partially squashed by the tire of some car or truck.

It wasn't long after my find that I also found a nice place a bit off the road to pull over and make a small campfire. It was a beautiful and calm spot with stars shining above. I felt at peace, alone with my thoughts, my natural surroundings, and the squirrel. I skinned the squirrel, which looked way smaller without fur. I joked to myself about making a tiny hat from the skin, but instead just gutted it and stuck it on a stick. It could have tasted much better with any type of sauce or even salt, but having nothing and being quite ravenously hungry at the time, it tasted great. I decided that road kill would be on the menu for the rest of my trip.

The next night, after poking about ten animals, none of which were fresh, I finally found a fresh possum that would be my next meal. It was much larger than the tiny squirrel, but I must not have been as hungry because it certainly didn't taste as good.

That evening wasn't quite the same as the perfect serene solitude of the night before. I also had a very hard time finding a place to sleep. I finally ended up quite a way off the road, down a narrow dirt path, and at a small creepy cemetery. The trees covered my view of the stars, and a thin fog even rolled in. I should have found a better place, but I stayed and passed a mostly sleepless, freaked-out night.

When I got to Atlanta and saw its beautiful skyline, it was strange to be back in a big city. I found a payphone and called a friend I had met a few years earlier. She invited me out, so I met her at Café Tutu Tango in Buckhead. We had a blast catching up. She paid for our dinner and drinks, and I had a bed to sleep in for the first time in a few days, which was nice as well. Seeing those we don't often get to see during our normal routines is one of my favorite things about being out on the road.

Leaving late the next morning, it should have been an easy day getting back to Charlottesville, but I was slowed by two things. First, I picked up a hitchhiker who needed to get to Raleigh, North Carolina. This was way out of my way, but I had never gone that direction before, so I agreed to take him. Then he smoked a joint and got paranoid about me driving my normal ninety miles per hour and insisted that I stay within four miles per hour above the speed limit. I wasn't in a hurry, and he was quite insistent that cops would pull me over going any faster, so I obliged. Bill Parsley, the hitchhiker, was an older man with a lot of good stories about his hobo life. I was actually sad when I dropped him off at a rundown duplex where his friend lived.

As soon as old Mr. Parsley was out of the car, I was back to racing along the freeway. It was getting late, and being alone with myself for so long, I began playing games in my head. One of the games almost killed me. I was thinking about Einstein's relativity and I imagined not that my car was speeding forward along the freeway, but that my vehicle was in one place, and the Earth was spinning at the speed of my vehicle below me. It was a really cool sensation as if I were sitting still, driving a video game. Then I took it one step further and turned the Earth upside-down in my head, so I was driving on the bottom of the spinning Earth. Immediately I lost orientation and all perspective was gone. Luckily it was about midnight, and there were no cars anywhere around me because I lost control. The car began swerving wildly back and forth across the three lanes of the freeway. I had to dodge some big orange road construction cones in the middle and sides of the road. I finally slowed down and straightened the car into one lane. I didn't play that game while driving again.

Having arrived back to Charlottesville at about 3 am, I realized that I still had a bit of the Jack Daniels left. I decided that I couldn't go home without finishing it. I headed to my friend Edy's house instead. Edy's boyfriend didn't like me very much. He didn't understand that Edy and my relationship was spiritual, intellectual, and playful, and not sexual. The closest we ever came to a physical relationship was after one of Edy's parties. We were the last two left and high on martinis and champagne. Edy painted a large eagle across my bare chest, and I painted tribal designs on hers.

I think the main reason Edy's boyfriend didn't like me was because one weekend while he was away, Edy was staying at his house and wanted to iron and sew a large twelve-inch patch of an eagle with upturned wings and a skull below it onto my riding jeans jacket. She did the ironing of the patch on his living room floor. When we pulled the jacket up, we discovered she had burned the perfect shape of the eagle and skull into his large Persian rug. When we saw the horribly obvious black shape burned onto the carpet, we looked at each other in shock. But there was nothing we could do but laugh. Edy's boyfriend never said anything to me about it, but he certainly hated seeing me in the jacket after that.

When I got to Edy's house, I didn't know if her boyfriend was around or not, so I quietly tapped on her bedroom window. She came out.

"What are you doing?" she asked quietly through the front door.

"I just got back from Alabama," I explained excitedly, "and I still have a bit of Jack Daniels left. I can't go home until it is done."

Without even questioning, Edy responded, "Okay, let's go for a drive."

Once in the car and a few blocks from her house, we quit whispering and took small swigs from the large JD bottle, passing it back and forth. I told her a bit about the trip, and she told me about her weekend. We began joking, laughing, and really having a great time. It was a party of two rolling down the country roads in Virginia.

I was in mid-laugh over something when "Sweet Home Alabama" came on the radio. I yelled, "Yes!" With my right hand, I turned the volume up. With my left, I grabbed my nickel-plated, 7.5-inch .44 Magnum and fired it up into the air through the open driver's side window. A shocking explosion of sound cracked through the silence of the woods and echoed across a large field.

Edy was shaken and even mad for a moment. She demanded, "Give me the gun," which I did, and she didn't let me have it back.

Once I explained that it was the last firework to celebrate the finish line of my adventure, she quickly got back into the spirit of things.

When Edy was getting out of my car as the sun was just starting to rise, she noticed a duck lying on a newspaper on the floor of the back seat.

"A duck," she noted, picking it up. "Awesome, I'll cook it for you."

"That would be great," I said. We made plans for dinner at her house for that evening.

In the middle of the amazing meal, Edy asked, "Where'd you get the duck?"

"In Alabama," I answered.

"Did you go hunting?"

"No."

"Did someone give it to you?" she continued.

"No."

"Then where did you get it?"

"I found it," I replied.

"Where?" Edy questioned slowly, starting to look suspicious.

"Uh," I started. Then I managed, "In the middle of the road." I looked up at Edy, hoping this wouldn't spoil the great dinner we were sharing.

"You have got to be kidding me," Edy uttered, still with a small bite of duck in her mouth. "Are you telling me this is road kill? Are you telling me that I just cooked a gourmet road kill duck?"

"Yes," I confirmed, now giggling.

After the initial surprise, Edy was fine finishing the lovely meal, which had quickly turned entirely more funny than elegant.

## *About You*

Have you ever had a unique friendship with someone, a friendship that was somehow different from most others? Who was it with, and what made it special?

Reflect on the various types of friendships. From exercise and cafe friends to work friends and friends from childhood, there exist many variations on friendship. What particular rewards does each type of friendship give?

Do Something Extraordinary

Think of a person you'd like to become even better friends with. Plan a time to spend with them and prior to seeing them, create a list of things you can do to make the time together extra special and memorable.

# FIVE

# COLORADO SPRINGS SOFA

*Colorado, USA. 1996. Twenty-Seven Years Old*

Wind-blown and full of dust, I rolled into Colorado Springs at dusk. I had a name—Mark —and was looking forward to the sheltered comfort of his sofa. Mark was still a name to me, not yet a friend, but we had partied hard together a few days earlier in Minneapolis.

"You should come down an' see me in Colorado Springs," he said emphatically as he lowered his mug of beer to the table. His drunk attention turned to his wife who, with another girl at the table, was dancing "La Margarita," or whatever that song was called. She had been in LA for the past few months, and Mark wondered how she had learned the dance, considering that she wasn't supposed to be going out. His jealousy took control, and he began paying more attention to her.

By the end of the night, however, Mark had mentioned me coming to Colorado Springs a few more times. When we parted ways at 4:30 in the morning, I had his number scribbled on a scrap of paper in my pocket.

I rode hard, sleeping one night in some back woods in Missouri and making it to Colorado in two days. There was an early morning storm in Missouri, so it rained heavily on me as I slept. I was drunk enough that the rain didn't wake me, but when lightning nearly struck my scooter, I sprang up like a cat. Unconsciously, my hand twisted under my leather jacket pillow, feeling for the .44 Mag, which should have been there, but had gotten stolen two days earlier.

Maybe it was a good thing the gun had been stolen, maybe not. In either case, in Kentucky, the night following the theft, I was spooked awake by one of Kentucky's finest. The dumb fool should know better than to spook a sleeping man next to his chopper at four in the morning. There is a reason bikers don't sleep at Motel 6 all the time. Part of the time it is because they don't have $29.50 for a room, and other times it is simply because they don't want to be around people. This was one of these nights.

It had been dark for about an hour and raining lightly, so I pulled off 65 North, filled my peanut tank, and bought a six-pack of canned Budweiser. I wasn't too far north of some city, so I asked a teenager where a good place to bunk down might be. Being a teenager, he knew of some doozies, but most of them seemed like the soggy clearings found under wide trees just inside some small woods, places that usually included at least six old beer cans and bottles, at least one washing machine lid or part of some other large white appliance, and at least the centerfold of a wet Playboy whose pages were all stuck together. Finally, the teen pointed me in the direction of an abandoned grade school. Not that I had anything against the first options he provided, for I also occasionally spent time sneaking out to find peace and refuge in such places, but I opted for the school. It was just about right, a little too close to suburbia for my taste, but there were some trees to hide behind and a lawn to sleep on.

All was well until officer friendly popped in for a visit. I sprang out of my sleep, and the cop pulled his gun on me. I didn't care. I knew he wouldn't shoot me as soon as I realized he was a cop. He made me climb out of my Mexican blanket and walk all over the wet grass in my socks while he started digging through my stuff.

"Listen, Officer," I said speaking English in a way I thought he could relate to. "I ain't got no drugs, and I ain't got no gun. I'm just traveling through, not wantin' to bother anybody and not wantin' to be bothered."

My switchblade was sticking out of my rear pants pocket on the ground right in front of the cop, but that was about the only thing he didn't see. Those little knives are tricky though. Until you need 'em you forget about them. That happened to me at the Sea-Tac Airport once. They didn't arrest me, but "detained" me for about forty minutes. They also warned me not to try to get onto a plane with one again.

I remember pleading with the airport officer, "I swear it won't happen again. I'm just on my way up to Alaska for some work. I didn't know the knife was in my bag."

I hadn't known either. When the alarm first sounded, I thought it was due to a meatloaf that I had wrapped in tinfoil. When I began digging through the pack though, the lady at the X-ray machine pushed the panic button.

A swarm of middle-aged security guards and cops sprinted my way. The panic could have been for anyone in the area, which was quite crowded, but they grabbed me first. I guess it was my black cowboy hat.

When they were finished, I asked for the blade back, again explaining that I was just passing through Seattle on my way to Alaska.

"Listen, partner," the cop said. "This little knife is illegal in all fifty states, so the fact that you are passing through or not is irrelevant. I could bust you big." He didn't give the knife back.

I pulled off the highway at the first pay phone I saw in Colorado Springs. It took me a while to find the scrap of paper with Mark's number on it in my soggy wallet.

"Hello."

"Hey, is Mark around?"

"No."

"Is he still in Minneapolis?"

"He's not back yet."

I proposed that since I knew Mark, I might come over anyway, but the reception was not enthusiastic. The guy at the end of the line sounded stiff and even told me that he was about to have dinner with his girlfriend. What a blow. I'd really wanted to sleep on a sofa.

Annoyed, I said I would come by later, at about 10:30 pm when Mark would be back.

What to do? I rode for a while looking for a Denny's, or a similar restaurant, at which I could rest my bum while sipping stale coffee for 3.5 hours. I couldn't find one. My options ranged from Burger King to pizza parlors. Since I wanted to be served, Burger King was out. Since I knew I didn't have much cash, pizza was out.

As I was exploring near the mountain side of the city, a bike passed me. I did a wide U-turn and followed it to a small bar with six motorcycles on the curb.

"You found the right place," the guy said as he and his girl dismounted a chopper. I followed the bearded vet into Smoothies.

"Can I buy you a beer?" I asked.

"Sure."

"Two Buds," I announced to the bartender.

Sizing up the room as I walked in, I noticed some motorcycle club patches. As I turned to order the beer, I intentionally exposed my back, revealing that I wasn't wearing a rocker underneath the winged patch on my back.

Then I turned toward my new friend, asking, "What's your name?" At the same time, I held out my hand.

"Dan," he growled and firmly gripped my hand.

After the introduction, I realized that I didn't have any dough.

"Sorry, Dan. All's I got is a buck." I held the dollar bill up showing him my empty billfold chained to my belt. I truly intended to buy Dan a beer. I didn't realize how strapped I was.

"Don't worry, man, I'll buy you a beer then." Dan knew the barmaid, so he laboriously wrote a check for cash, like it was the first one he had ever written, and handed me an ice-cold beer in a tall glass.

It hit me just right. I toasted his glass and drank half of the beer on my first taste. Because I hadn't eaten all day and was tired from the windy ride through Kansas, I was slightly buzzed off the first beer.

After being introduced to most of the patch-holders in the place, someone screamed something, and Dan asked if I wanted to run out to Bony Bitches with them. I said, "Sure," and we aggressively funneled toward the small front exit.

Not knowing the pecking order, I watched Dan for clues. He kicked on his Panhead and told me he would take up the rear, so I wouldn't get lost. I pulled onto the street in second-to-last position.

The ride over to Bony Bitches was quite a race. There were eight of us throttling hard, even through red stoplights. Our thunderous presence was unavoidable. At one point, the pack split up. That was when the real race began. We met up with the three "short-cutters" about ten minutes later as we roared past them at a stoplight doing about a hundred. I felt tentative riding so close to the front of the pack, being an outsider, so I slid back to the rear.

Upon arriving at Bony Bitches, we pulled our bikes around back. I was told that the owner was a big, one-legged biker, and that the place was rarely a flop.

Realizing that I still didn't have any dough, I told Dan that I had to go find a cash machine. I usually called them "slot machines" though. They were great because, unlike the ones in Vegas, I almost always won. Tonight, however, was different. I rode about a mile and a half before finding a bank. I slipped my card in, but either I wasn't getting my secret number right, or I didn't have any money in it to win.

Then, as I was digging through my wallet, a miracle happened. I saw the edge of a greenback stuffed way deep behind all the pockets. As I unfolded the thin wad, I found that it was a ten and a twenty, with a note attached that read: *To my buddy, in case he needs some extra cash. Love, Kelly.* Kelly was the girl I had left in Virginia about a week earlier on this one-way trip to LA.

An arrow hit me in the stomach, and I smiled so hard that my half-lid helmet felt tight. I stuffed the paper into my vest pocket and throttled strong, excited to return to the tavern.

I made it back in seconds and walked in with a smile. As I approached the bar, I noticed an enormous mug of beer. Dan slid it toward me, and I gulped it strongly, allowing my face to become wet with foam. Then I told him of my miracle and showed him the yellow note.

"You should keep that one," he remarked. "There aren't many good enough to do that."

The next round, I bought, and we drank to Kelly, whom I bragged about during the entire beer and maybe a little more.

"I'm starved!" I declared once I realized it. "What have you got to eat in this place?" I asked Toni, the barmaid.

"Nothin' but frozen burritos and stuff like that," she answered. "You don't want to eat that shit."

"Yes, I do!" I exclaimed. "Frozen burritos and hot dogs are my staple."

"Are you hungry?" Toni inquired, eyeing me curiously.

"Yes!" I responded emphatically with a smile on my face.

"Then drink this." Toni poured one shot of Tequila followed by one shot of some other drink that tasted like pepperoni.

"Right on," I said as I finished the shots. My hunger was immediately cured.

We partied hard for a while. Toni was not shy about her interest in me. I was amazed later when I went to the bathroom. I looked in the faded mirror to see a dirty head with bugs and bees still stuck to my face. I chuckled as I washed myself and dried with my bandanna. I was a new man: no better, no worse, just cleaner.

When I walked out, Toni was the only one who noticed. She was with a guy named Hal, who was showing her his back full of tattoos. Although I also marveled at the tattoos, Toni's attention was enough to swoon his rivalry.

I placed myself on a stool and struck up a conversation with a truck driver from Virginia. He offered me a job unloading for him. I took his number and told him that I would call him at 6:30 am, but the job was not destined to be.

Once Hal was called away, Toni, who had been listening peripherally to me and the truck driver, leaned over the bar squashing her breast against the back of my hand. She whispered that she lived alone and that I could stay over at her place if I wanted. I immediately began to get excited. Blood began to rush through my body, but before I could answer, Dan yelled something about going to another bar. I looked at Toni. Her cute, short blonde hair and her large eyes. I leaned over and kissed her firmly on the mouth.

"I gotta go," I said. Toni walked around the bar and slid up to me. I began to hug her when Hal came up behind her squeezing her between the two of us in a mighty hug.

"Take us both!" he roared, as he picked her up and me with her.

"Bye," I said as Toni leaned forward kissing me again. Our eyes locked for a moment in a questioning stare. She wanted me to stay: for a night, a week, a year. She didn't seem to care.

Once again, we were screaming through the streets. Hal and I dragged two stoplights laying long streaks of rubber on the road. I won, but I let him slide by me both times when the sprint was finished. I didn't know where we were and felt lost, but we ended up at some karaoke bar. The music was great. I became infatuated while listening to renditions of Led Zeppelin and Meatloaf.

Then it began to happen.

Hal approached, mumbling, "Jerk," under his breath.

"What's up?" I asked.

"Nothing. Just the little fucker over there bumped into me with his elbow. Not obvious enough for me to know if it was an accident or not."

"I got your back if something happens," I assured him.

"No. It's nothing."

I went to the restroom and while taking a long piss, one of the guys from another big group walked in. He was with the guy who had bumped Hal. I could tell they were looking for trouble. I eyed the guy with the corner of my vision, ready to react to any attack. *I can take him*, I thought to myself, and I became aware of every object in the small bathroom that could be used as a weapon. I would bash his head against the urinal or the sink, I decided. It was tense. I washed my hands slowly as he stood above one of the toilets in the stall unsuccessfully trying to piss, then I walked out.

I rejoined the table and drank more beer until I saw the standoff. Three men were accusing Hal of hitting on one of their women. They were looking for an excuse to fight. I jumped up from my chair and stood at Hal's side. I judged the distance so that no one could headbutt me in the face, as had happened to me before. I felt for the knife in my back pocket. I let the blade remain but felt confident by the fact that she was there.

The guy from the bathroom walked by, nudging me with his elbow as he passed, like he was drunk and wobbly. Was it an accident? He was small, but his physical contact was enough to ignite an already tense situation. As we stood face-to-face with a group of large, tough-looking men who greatly outnumbered us, I imagined the whole fight. I was front and center to the confrontation, visualizing Hal smacking the largest of their group.

In my mind, I saw the whole fight play out. I would hit the guy next to Hal. The small guy would swing at me, hitting me in the side of the head. Hal would attack him. *As they grappled, others from our crew joined the fight. I pushed them into three guys and then went for the tall, skinny one. It became a frenzy of punching, grabbing, and scrambling. I got control over the tall guy and brought him to the ground by pulling on his long hair. I kneed him in his abdomen and then head. He was out of the fight, so I headed back into the confusion.*

During the face-off, the president of the club I was with had now positioned himself at the front of the confrontation, with Hal to his left and me to his right. He nodded that I should get out of the situation, but I stayed. Next, he began confidently describing to the giant leader of the other group what would happen if we were to go to blows. He said that he hoped we actually would and that we would not show any mercy.

As I stood facing the menacing group, the adrenaline rush that only predatory animals and fighters feel kicked in. Though greatly outsized and outnumbered, I saw us tear them apart. I think everyone on their side saw this too. As they looked into our eyes, they saw something that broke them before a punch was thrown.

Taking advantage of his momentarily relaxed state, the president said to the other group, "Your call." Their leader only needed to take one small step backward on the beer-soaked floor for the situation to end. There was no less hatred among them, but they were too scared to act upon it.

After the standoff, I hurried to the entrance to find a guy near our bikes looking guilty. It was obvious that he was about to trash one of our bikes.

"What the hell are you doing?" I spouted. I sprang towards the guy thinking that I would have to chase him, but he didn't move. He began to walk toward me, and I put my hands up ready to fight.

"What the fuck?" Dan shouted as he and the rest of the crew filed out of the front door of the bar.

Fight averted by the sudden numbers on my side, I took a breath of relief and met my new friends. Sucking air and ready to puke because of the jolt of adrenaline and a bit too much beer, I forced a smile and commented, "Hell of a party."

After hugging each other and celebrating that we had beaten the will of a tough group of guys who'd tried to mess with us, I tied my bandana to the bottom of my ape-hangers and waited for the riders to roll out ahead of me.

"No," called out the president of the club, standing up, straddling his Harley, and pointing. "You're not in back this time. You're riding right up front next to me for this one." It was a remarkable token of respect, which I gladly accepted and appreciated.

We rode in two columns slowly back to Bony Bitches. Back at the tavern, we commenced to drink more beer. I had hoped Toni would still be there, but she had left.

Once the adrenaline ran off, I was again drunk, but at a low. Even the beer was difficult to drink. I sipped my bitter-tasting Bud, fighting nausea for about twenty minutes before I began to feel my old self again. We recounted the confrontation over and over, acting it out in front of drunk and excited spectators, until about 4:30 when Dan, with his wife under his arm, told me, "Come on, we're going. You can sleep on my sofa if you want."

"That's what I wanted to hear, man," I said. "That's all I came to Colorado Springs for," and we walked lazily toward our bikes.

As we fired up the bikes and began riding back to Dan's house, it was getting chilly in the early morning crispness of the mountain town. We were not racing like we had been doing earlier. I was, at this point, feeling very tired, but I was immediately sparked awake when I heard a gunshot.

Dan was way in front of me. I didn't know where the shot had come from, but I thought somehow the group that we had gotten into a massive confrontation with earlier had followed us and wanted revenge. Dan turned left into a neighborhood, and I crouched down as low as I could, making myself a smaller target for the next shot. However, when I pulled left into the street, my bike slid out from under me. I realized that we weren't being shot at. The explosive crack was my motorcycle's threadbare rear tire bursting.

Dan continued and turned into a house about a half-block away, so I just rode slowly and as carefully as I could on the flat tire. Dan's garage was already open, so I pulled in and showed him what had happened.

As we walked into the house, Dan's wife asked, "Where are the dogs?" I would later learn that Dan's wife was having some issues with a crazy ex-boyfriend. When we entered the house, she could tell that something wasn't right.

Dan pulled out a semiautomatic pistol from the small of his back and began clearing the house. It was as if Dan, the war veteran, were back in Vietnam. He rolled down the hallway, kicking open closets. Then he'd combat roll into a bedroom with pistol drawn. We checked every room and closet, but the house was empty.

Then Dan's wife saw the blinking light on the telephone answering machine, and we learned that the dogs had gotten out but were safe with a neighbor for the night.

Dan's wife laid out a sheet and a blanket for me on the puffy brown sofa in their living room. I welcomed the much-needed rest. It felt so good to be warm and comfortable on a nice soft couch. It was about 5:30 in the morning. As soon as my head hit the pillow, I drifted off to sleep.

At 8:00 am, Dan's wife shook my shoulder to wake me. I was still in a deep sleep and had only been on the sofa for 2.5 hours. Dan's wife told me that Dan had already left for work and that my bike was at the Harley shop. She'd drop me off on her way to work. I didn't bother showering but just put on my jeans and t-shirt. We walked out to her car.

When we got to the dealership, it was still only about 8:30 in the morning. When I walked in, one of the guys told me, "All done, partner."

"What is?" I asked.

"Your bike," he continued. "Dan had us pick it up from his house this morning, and the tire's fixed."

I was in disbelief that they'd replaced the tire so quickly. It definitely wasn't the experience I'd had at other dealerships I'd been to.

"Awesome," I responded and walked over to the counter where the guy was standing. I pulled out my billfold and asked, "How much?"

"Nothing, man," the guy continued as one of the mechanics rolled my bike from the service area and out to the front parking lot.

I was shocked. "Wow," I said, "I can't thank you enough. I really appreciate it."

"That's how we do things here," the guy said. "It is all about taking care of a brother." Dan obviously told him about what had happened the night before and how I had been willing to fight in the trenches alongside his motorcycle club.

I felt a profound joy. The joy had nothing to do with saving a hundred and fifty bucks for a new tire. It was out of respect for the way they were helping me and due to my witnessing the brotherhood of riders in action.

I shook hands and hugged the three guys who were in the shop. Next, I walked out to my bike. I threw my leg over, still a bit groggy from the hard drinking and lack of sleep. I pulled out into the cool morning looking forward to a wonderful day of riding and wondering who else I might meet on the rest of my ride from Virginia to LA.

## About You

Have you ever been rewarded unexpectedly for doing something to help others? What happened and how did it feel?

Why might joining clubs or groups be healthy for people? Do you know of anyone who has grown and changed in a positive way due to their participation in a club or group?

Do Something Extraordinary

Think about a club or group, formal or informal, that is interesting to you. Spend a bit of time learning about it and explore whether joining might be a good idea. Keep doing this until you find a club or group that makes you excited to join.

# SIX

# VIRGINITY

*Paris, France. 1994. Twenty-Four Years Old*

Her name was Sabine. She was stunning: tall, strawberry-blonde hair, full lips, and equally as beautiful with or without her large red glasses on.

The first time I saw Sabine was at the Mustang Café on Boulevard du Montparnasse. I was with Dave, a friend from the USA, who was visiting me in Paris for a week.

It was an exceptionally energetic night. Some girls were even dancing on tables to an up-beat jazzy-funk song that was hitting popularity at the time. Dave and I first stopped by the Piano Vache, a quirky café club that I sometimes visited. To show Dave as much of Paris as I could, we ended up in Montparnasse.

I first saw Sabine from across the room. It was hard to miss her. She was with a group of three girls and three guys. It was obvious that there was one guy in particular who was directing most of his attention toward Sabine. He was tall with short brown hair. His air of arrogance was cracked only by his obvious responsiveness to all of Sabine's actions.

At one point, on the way to order Dave and myself another beer, I ended up face-to-face with the stunning woman from across the bar. We were both squeezing between people in the crowded aisle and almost bumped into each other as we were passing in different directions. We both smiled at the unintended closeness.

Up close, she smelled wonderful. Her skin glowed as she said, *"Pardon,"* and I said, *"Excusez moi,"* in my American accent. I was enchanted. She smiled generously.

After returning with the beers, I rushed back to Dave to tell him of my encounter. My heart raced, and my stomach was filled with butterflies. No other person in the lively club now mattered. I had to do something. Knowing that my chances were slim, I asked the bartender for a pen, wrote my phone number on a small square napkin, and waited for the right opportunity.

As the beautiful woman was again in the crowded aisle of people, I took a sip of my beer, engendering as much courage as I could. I quickly headed in her direction as if I were passing to use the toilet, which was down the stairs just past her. In my head, I was rehearsing what I would say. As I passed, I leaned in close to her lovely ear and said in awkward French, "I understand you are with someone tonight, but if you want to, give me a call tomorrow." As I said this, I slipped the napkin into her hand. I glanced back while walking away and saw her staring at the napkin with neither a smile nor disgust.

I decided that I would not approach the girl again for the rest of the night, but I bored Dave to death by speaking about nothing else. I was infatuated with her. Much later in the evening, her group ended up next to Dave and me, and we began speaking.

"*Je suis Sabine*," she said first.

"*Mon nom est Erik*," I responded, pronouncing my name with my most French accent of "ehr-eek" as it sounded when French people said it.

Much later at about one in the morning, one of Sabine's friends invited Dave and me to go have coffee with them. Even though Dave was patiently waiting for us to leave, I eagerly accepted. Sabine's group of boys and girls and Dave and I ended up sitting at a large table with coffees in front of us. Dave, who had just arrived in Paris, was a tired mess, but I needed him to distract the group, so I could have a chance to privately ask Sabine out. He rose to the occasion by distracting them with conversation, and Sabine accepted my invitation for a date.

Since we had missed the last metro of the night, Dave and I had a long walk back to my apartment in the 15th arrondissement. He was a walking zombie from the effects of beer, jetlag, and total lack of sleep, but I was excited. I floated along the Champ de Mars under the trees near the Eiffel Tower as we made our way home. The birds were singing, and the sun was beginning to light the beautiful city.

A month later and Sabine and I were a couple. We'd spend afternoons at sidewalk cafés drinking espresso and smoking cigarettes at tiny round tables. We'd spend our weekends out late at the Mustang Café or other clubs.

On one Friday night, our normal routine of splitting up at a metro platform with a long kiss did not occur. Rather, I found myself walking back to my small apartment with Sabine on my arm. We strolled across the same park Dave and I had traversed the first night I'd met her. We chatted casually, and the closer to my apartment we got, the more distracted I became with anticipation for where we were going. As we walked down my apartment's tiny hardwood floor hallway toward the bedroom door at its end, my body already began to react to how much I looked forward to being close to Sabine in my bed.

I think we were both nervous as we entered. We took off our clothes down to our underwear before crawling into the tiny bed together. The sheets felt cool in contrast to our warm bodies. Sabine's skin was as smooth as it looked. We locked in a tight embrace. Sabine took off her brassiere, and we kissed. I held the sides of her head with my hands and stared into her large hazel eyes. From inches away, we alternated kissing and staring at each other. I was in love, and I didn't want it to end. When Sabine took off her underwear, my excitement was almost overwhelming.

As Sabine looked up from under me, her hair surrounding her head on the pillow as if she were an angel, she said, "Let's make love."

Still looking into her eyes, I responded, "No."

The lovely tone of Sabine's face didn't change, but the look in her eyes was one of perplexed confusion.

"*Pourquoi?*" Sabine asked curiously.

The decision not to have sex with Sabine in this situation, in which I was already loosened up by a number of drinks and slightly mentally hampered by tiredness after a full night out, would have been an extremely difficult one if I hadn't already made the decision not to have sex years before this pivotal moment. It had been probably five years earlier that I simply decided not to have sex with anyone until I was married. It was an idealistic gift that I wanted to give to the future person whom I'd meet and ultimately marry.

"I made a decision to wait until marriage," I explained to Sabine.

We spent the rest of the night embracing and kissing, but my boxer shorts stayed on.

The next morning Sabine sat shirtless on the edge of my bed, as the sun shone on her through my seventh-story window. While making coffee, I marveled at the perfection of her whole body. However, as she stared out the window, I could tell that something small had changed. I hated the thought of what it could be.

Over the coming weeks, as Sabine became more and more distant, it was one of Sabine's friends who told me, "Sabine needs '*un homme*,'" or "Sabine needs A MAN," emphatically insisting that sex was a part of a relationship that Sabine couldn't live without.

At this point, Sabine and I were still considered a couple, so our standard Parisian greeting was a small kiss on the lips when we saw each other rather than the typical kiss on both cheeks as is done by friends.

That evening I had a rendezvous with Sabine and a few of her friends. From time to time, I'd meet new friends of Sabine, and I could tell that my being American was part of the charm that she enjoyed showing off. As I approached the group waiting at the café, I could tell Sabine was in a cheerful mood. There was already wine poured.

As I walked up to Sabine, she stood. I greeted her with a kiss on each cheek … not a peck on the lips. It was obvious to all at the table what had just happened. Sabine looked at me with perplexed confusion similar to what I'd seen in bed a few weeks earlier.

After kissing all the others in the group on the cheek during introductions, I sat next to Sabine. As a group, we spoke about amusing things, and I affectionately held Sabine's hand during the evening, but that was the end of the romantic relationship with this amazing, beautiful person whom I desperately adored.

## About You

*Have you ever been totally infatuated with someone, but there was something that kept you apart? Who was it and how did it make you feel?*

*What are some reasons people become infatuated with others? What constitutes physical or mental beauty to you?*

*Do Something Extraordinary*

*If you are single, make a bold move to show someone with whom you are infatuated that you have feelings for them. If you have a partner, make a list of things that attracted you to them at the beginning of the relationship and that attract you to them currently. Share the list with them. Also, reconstruct moments from when you initially met to rekindle the passionate feelings of new love.*

# SEVEN

# REFLECTIONS ON BELONGING

While thinking about how a sense of belonging helped me find meaning, it becomes evident that there are different manifestations of belonging. In my experiences, I felt an overwhelming sense of belonging from very brief but powerful one-time encounters, from sustained and nurtured long-term relationships, and from communities, cultures, and sub-cultures that allowed me to feel a sense of fulfillment from their accepting me into their respective worlds.

When I reflect on Onawa's wide smile, I am warmed by the overwhelming sense of love we shared. It wasn't a lustful love. Sitting with Onawa in front of a small campfire was filled with an absolute pouring out of emotions. We belonged with each other. Even though the situation was ephemeral, we both benefited from our beautiful, yet fleeting, sharing of paths. I know that for myself thoughts of this wonderful encounter have surfaced many times. Each time I'm filled with positive sensations that will always be linked to wonderful moments like this, moments that went beyond ordinary and live in the world of extraordinary.

My relationships with Edy while a grad-student in Virginia and with Sabine while living in Paris were also built upon a foundation of belonging. One was based on a profound, special friendship and the other upon a romantic attraction. In both circumstances, there was an important frequency in our interactions. We were able to go beyond the line of superficial and into a powerful, sustained interaction, which provided an extremely comforting level of connection. We belonged to each other. The quality of my time in both Virginia and in Paris was profoundly enhanced by these beautiful connections.

Notice that these connections didn't occur randomly. I created these by allowing myself to become emotionally close to a platonic friend and by taking a big risk in revealing to Sabine my initial crush on her. In both situations the "safe" thing would have been for me to stay away from Edy based on her boyfriend's wishes or to admire Sabine from afar without taking action. I'm oh-so happy that I did neither since my connection with these amazing individuals has had a lasting positive impact on my life.

As I feel excited while reflecting on belonging with individual people, I also feel wonderful when I think about my time with the Wayana Indians, the Berber tribe in Morocco, and the bikers in Colorado. I could not have survived in the Amazon without the Wayana accepting me. The more time I spent with them and the more I learned about their culture, the more I began to feel I belonged with them. In both South America and Africa, I experienced the same progression of emotions going from total excitement to loneliness to feeling acceptance and love. Because of my eagerness to learn the culture, be friendly, and help others, I was loved in return. When I reached a critical sense of belonging, my time with them became wonderfully meaningful.

During my life and travels, I hadn't realized that I needed to feel a sense of belonging, but as I look back, I understand how profoundly belonging affected me. In the past, I cared for the people I connected with. I loved first, and the result was a positive for me as well as extraordinary connections were formed. Now that I understand how powerfully important belonging has been in my life, I try to consciously construct connections with others, and I'm delighted how both I and others profit from it.

Returning to Esfahani Smith's book, she writes:

The search for meaning is not a solitary philosophical quest … and meaning is not something that we create within ourselves and for ourselves. Rather, meaning largely lies in others. Only through focusing on others do we build the pillar of belonging for both ourselves and for them. If we want to find meaning in our own lives, we have to begin by reaching out.

## *About You*

*How could you reach out or open yourself up to another individual, club, association, or group to improve the sense of belonging in your life? Extraordinary connections are waiting for you.*

*At the end of each narrative, I shared a simple task that might add a greater sense of belonging to your life. I hope you enjoyed these exercises. The next step is to select a few of them and put them into routine practice until they become habits that weave positive connections into your life and help build up the pillar of belonging within you.*

*If you feel like adding one more connection to your life, I'd love to hear from you. You can contact me directly at Erik@ErikSeversen.com.*

# PART 2

# PURPOSE

*The ability to find purpose in the day-to-day tasks of living and working goes a long way toward building meaning.*

—Emily Esfahani Smith

# EIGHT

## HAY FOR THE COWS

*Kent Grandma's House, USA. 1995.*
*Twenty-Five Years Old*

"Oh, I can feed the cows, Grandma," I said, as I saw the youthful 88-year-old putting on her brown coat.

"No, no, you do your studies," my grandma instructed, pausing to confirm that the exchange was over.

"I can do it," I pressed. I actually welcomed the break from my thick literature book. Plus, I knew that although she was very capable of feeding the cows twice a day as she had been doing for years, Grandma preferred to stay in the kitchen cooking.

"Do you want to?" she asked tentatively.

"Yes!"

"Okay, but watch your step."

My grandmother always reminded me of her feeding-the-cows routine before I went out even though I'd done it hundreds of times. She couldn't help herself. She took great pride in taking care of her cows and her huge vegetable garden.

Grandma continued, "Give them only the hay that is untied; you can see for yourself. And make sure you give Bossy the oats." There was always one cow named Bossy. Because Bossy was always next in line for the following year's dinner table, Bossy got a bit more food and extra attention.

"Okay," I responded. I grabbed a handful of peanuts, stuffed them into my faded tan hunting jacket, and walked across the large yellow-and-white kitchen toward the back door.

"No, you can't go out, Blacky," I uttered, pushing the thin black cat back with the side of my foot as I slid through the partially opened door and into the crisp morning. It was a perfectly clear day, and frost sparkled on the short grass. A thin layer of ice had formed in the small black wheelbarrow that stood by a flowerbed near the white picket fence.

As I stepped outside, I grabbed the tall walking stick that leaned against the house, crossed the yard, and slipped through the tiny white gate into the pasture.

I popped a few peanuts in my mouth as I sauntered toward the barn. I wasn't in a hurry. Right on cue, Billy, the Halison's dog, came sprinting across two large fields to greet me. Wagging the whole back half of his body to make his short tail wag more dramatically, he circled me excitedly with his tongue flapping out of his mouth. I patted Billy on the head and rubbed his back for a quick moment as I continued walking. He stayed next to me all the way to the barn. Billy had no idea that the cows didn't like him. He would try to play with them, but I think the cows thought he was a spaz.

When I reached the large white barn, I leaned in my weight to push open the heavy sliding door. I grabbed a pitchfork and scattered the hay into the feeding bins. The five cows were already lined up and angling their heads through the wooden slats to get to the hay.

As soon as they had seen me, they started walking toward the barn. I dipped the large, empty coffee can into the fifty-pound bag of oats near the stalls and emptied it in front of Bossy who flipped his head back and forth a few times to make sure none of the other cows tried to get into his space.

Most of the hay on the first floor was gone, so I climbed the built-in wooden ladder in the corner of the barn. We used the rough ladder often, but it always seemed to have cobwebs on it. Sun shone through the large opening at the end of the loft, lighting the speckles of sweet smelling hay, which hovered in the air.

I grabbed another pitchfork, which was leaning against the loft wall next to a large bag of rock salt, and pushed more loose hay down the small opening in the middle of the floor. Billy was still trying to figure out how to climb the ladder even after I was done. As I pulled the sliding barn door shut and latched it, I walked to the water trough, which was an old white bathtub. About a quarter-inch of ice had built up on the water from the cold night. I broke it up with the walking stick, so the cows could get to it.

Billy shot off as if he suddenly had something very important to do. I leaned down, pulling off a handful of the lush tall green grass that grew alongside the base of the tub. I walked over to the fence where the neighbor's horse was waiting for me. "Here you go, buddy," I said as I reached my hand through the fence, offering the grass to him. The dark brown horse's lips flapped against my palm as he gathered the grass off my hand.

I looked over at the giant pile of wood that needed to be chopped. I looked forward to getting started, but I'd wait until Monday. I noticed Mr. Halison at the far end of his farm. He was gathering eggs from his chicken coup. I waved to him.

As soon as I opened the back door to the house, Blacky the cat slipped out, but it didn't really matter. My grandma liked to keep Blacky inside most of the time, but Blacky would do what he wanted to do.

I took off my boots, hung my jacket, and walked back through the kitchen. It was 8:00 in the morning, and it was already a great day.

## *About You*

*Do you have any fond memories of simple day-to-day tasks that you did when you were young? What were they and what do you think of when you picture them?*

*What are some normal but meaningful tasks people do that they might take for granted?*

Do Something Extraordinary

*Think about a task you do every day or from time-to-time and consciously think about how it might be part of a bigger purpose than is immediately evident.*

# NINE

# MARONI RIVER

*French Guiana, South America. 1992.*
*Twenty-Three Years Old*

I had been up and down parts of the Maroni River separating French Guiana and Suriname many times, and I had become quite familiar with her. Commonly known as the Lawa River closer to the source near Brazil, the river is the lifeline for many Maroon and Amerindian tribes who live along her banks. For the Aluku, one of the tribes I spent a lot of time with while in South America, the water in the Maroni had almost supernatural powers. Often when one of the Aluku had to perform something requiring extreme strength, endurance, or even luck, they would submerge themselves in the river, allowing the energy of the water to transfer into them. The river, however, also wielded its powerful energy against people from time to time.

In one of my travels on the Maroni, I was with a group of Aluku in one large pirogue. We were traveling downstream after a hunting trip. At one point, our dugout canoe passed two small dugout canoes filled with Wayana

Indians. The canoes were composed of four people each and many other items—hammocks, bows and arrows, and large, flat cassava cakes. Some of the Wayana are seminomadic, and it was obvious that these people were moving everything they had to a different location along the river.

As the Wayana struggled upstream in their small packed canoes, we could tell that the river was beginning to force them into a shallower and more rapid section of its waters. As we passed them, we were concerned that they were entering real trouble as the rapids increased speed and intensity. Next the unthinkable happened: one of their canoes spun sideways in the rapids, was held up on a rock, and tipped over, spewing all its contents into the rushing water.

The screams we heard made us realize that it was much worse than just the materials getting swept downstream. A very young child, maybe two years old, was clinging to a bundle of hammocks in the rushing water. An adult Wayana who had been ejected from the boat began swimming as quickly as he could toward the baby, but he was going no faster than the rapids. The child's distance from him was expanding.

The Aluku in the boat I was in immediately pushed toward the shallower water to intercept the screaming infant. But the water became too shallow. We began grinding on boulders, and our thick wooden canoe began to spin. I was near the front, so with a rush of adrenalin, I flung myself into the rushing water. I desperately tried to pull myself along the boulders in the current toward where the infant would pass at any moment.

Fighting with all my might, I finally arrived in front of the bundle. The bundle hit me and knocked me over. As I fell backwards in the whitewater, I managed to grab the child and hold him firmly to my chest as the rushing water attempted to wrestle the slippery boy from my arms. I was still moving downstream, but it didn't take long for me to stop myself and work myself to a group of larger, secure boulders.

Once I was sure we had stopped, a wave of relief filled me. Then I began to shake with exhaustion. The child in my arms clung tightly to my neck, crying, but I could tell that even he knew that the worst was over.

As I was focusing on the child, the rest of the world disappeared. However, all the while I'd been in the water trying to catch him, the Aluku had been scrambling to help the rest of the Wayana. They secured the smaller boats of the Wayana alongside their larger canoe. They could see that I was in a safe spot, and once they stabilized themselves, they were able to come over to me and the frightened infant.

After prying his grip from my neck, I handed the shivering boy back to his terrified mother, who was standing in the twelve inches of water that filled her small canoe. She seemed too shocked to cry or communicate. As she hugged the naked child to her breasts and neck, she stared into my eyes, revealing her relief and gratitude.

* * *

A second incident with the Maroni—I was traveling upriver with a few Aluku and an Ndjuka named Naipon. We came to a *soula*, or small waterfall, about three feet tall. We would occasionally have to unload the canoe and carry it around falls, but there really wasn't a good place to do this along the steep banks of this small section of the river, so we decided to unload the canoe on a cluster of large rocks and pull the empty but still extremely heavy dugout canoe up the falls near the bank.

Bakos, one of the Aluku in our group, was directing the procedure. A few times already we'd tried to get the canoe over the boulders of the waterfall and past the rushing water, but hadn't quite made it. We decided to go for one more serious attempt. All four of us took our time gripping the rough rope as well as we could, and on a count of three, we pulled with all our might. Because I was the closest to the canoe, I could see that we were making progress. I strained and strained. We all did. The canoe was moving inch-by-inch.

Then Bakos yelled something in the Aluku language.

I thought that what Bakos shouted was words of encouragement, but I was wrong. In fact, he yelled, "Let go! It's not going to make it!"

I was the only one who didn't understand, so as all of the others abandoned the rope, I didn't let go. Immediately as the force of the water pushed the large canoe back down the fall, I was flung headfirst into the water below the *soula*. I didn't feel hurt from the fall, but I soon started to feel sharp, stabbing pains on my ankles and feet.

"Ouch!" I screamed, wondering what was happening, and then, "Ouch! ouch!" I continued as the razor-sharp pains continued.

I realized that I had cut my feet on the rocks as I fell in, and the blood was attracting piranhas. Every few seconds, I'd feel another bite tear into my flesh. As I stood up, even though I was only in waist-high water, the current was very strong and began pushing me over. To keep myself from getting swept away, I had to lower myself into the water and use my hands to crawl along the rocks toward the shore.

This is when Naipon's eyes got huge. He thought I was in trouble, so he jumped in. Although he was trying to save me, he belly-flopped right on my head, so instead of saving me, he about killed me.

After Naipon dragged me out of the water, we all began to laugh. We were laughing at how I'd been pulled into the river. We laughed at how I'd been smashed by Naipon. We even laughed at the eight small bleeding bite marks on my ankles.

After resting for a very long time on the large flat rocks near the side of the waterfall, one of the Aluku climbed to the bottom of the waterfall, held his breath, and submerged himself in the powerful water for about thirty seconds. Another one of the Aluku did the same thing.

"We're ready," they said.

On our next attempt, we pulled the pirogue over the falls and continued our journey up the Maroni River.

## *About You*

*Have you ever had to save someone? What happened, and how did you feel afterward?*

*Why do some people put themselves at risk to help another? Is it based on something random, like timing and circumstance, or something more profound, like personal ideology?*

Do Something Extraordinary

*Decide to assist people in need. Imagine three different scenarios where someone is in serious trouble, and you are the only one around to help. Imagine yourself acting right away, so if a situation ever comes up in real life, your mind is programed to help without pause.*

# TEN

# ONE DAY IN AFRICA

*Central African Republic. 1989. Twenty Years Old*

Fully rested, I opened my eyes and lay still for a moment, so I would not disturb the small drops of dew that coated me like a sheet. I smelled the fresh green grass growing around me and marveled at the pleasant sweet scent.

My first move was an unconscious one. I took my hand from its warm shelter inside my thin blue sleeping bag and ran it up my neck, stopping my fingers to scratch a small mosquito bite behind my ear.

A dog barked in the distance. I looked in the direction of the sun, which was not quite up yet. I did not have to look at my watch to know the time. I had opened my eyes like this at 5:30 in the morning every day for over a fortnight.

I slowly climbed out of my warm sleeping bag and into the crisp morning, exposing my naked body to a guard who sat in a chair at the edge of the yard. The guard chuckled to himself. He wasn't laughing at my nakedness but rather at my failing attempt to put on my wet clothes without stepping off my leather sandals, which were also wet and slippery with dew.

Once settled into my moist clothing, I gathered a few pieces of fruit and handed one to the guard before going into the communal house. Once inside I lit the kerosene stove, put on a pot of coffee, and sat down to peel a half-smashed mango.

"*Bon matin*, Erik," said a half-awake French woman who was as pretty in the morning as she was anytime.

"Good morning," I said as I watched her move into the kitchen dragging her slippers to attract attention to her long, thin legs. "Would you like some coffee?"

"*Oui*, it smells so good. Did you sleep outside again last night?"

"Yeah," I responded. "I can't afford 3,000 Central African Franks a night for a bed. I think I like it better out there anyway."

"You shouldn't. You'll get malaria, you know."

"No, I'll be fine," I answered as I poured her a cup of coffee, not knowing that I already had malaria. "Did you sleep well?"

"Okay, you?"

"Great," I responded truthfully.

Another girl came into the room and plopped down on a matted, rattan couch.

"Good morning, Lisa," I said, handing her a cup of coffee as well. Lisa was a Peace Corps volunteer from Georgia. Together we sat and drank for a time.

At a little before six, I slid my knife under my belt until it reached its comfortable and familiar position in the small of my back. The morning fog was just burning away, and I became slightly damp as I walked across the yard. I opened the rusted steel gate, nodded to the guard, and walked out into the Bangui morning. I did not know exactly where I was going, only that I was going to leave Africa soon, and I hadn't seen enough of it yet.

It was nice to sleep in a secure place, I thought to myself, without worrying about snakes, poachers, or any of the other unknowns that reside in the African wilderness. Although I no longer felt the oneness with nature that I had while alone in the jungle, I was well rested and happy with the day.

I walked quickly but easily through the dirt streets of Bangui, the capital of Central African Republic. I walked past a small tin-covered restaurant with a fire out front. There cooked *goso*, the playdough-like cassava, which is a staple food of the area. I smiled at the many people who looked at me strangely at first, then smiled in return. After a time, I saw a few soldiers with machine guns. I crossed the street to avoid any contact with them.

It was not long before I came upon the Ubangi River. I stood near its edge, scanning the surface in hopes of catching a glimpse of a hippopotamus or a crocodile. After buying a handful of peanuts from a small boy in a boat, I started to walk east along the river's edge. I walked slowly, enjoying the mild morning air, cherishing every breath, knowing that the damp coolness would turn to scorching heat later in the day.

It did not seem like long before I realized that the city of Bangui was far behind me. I also realized from the way I was walking that I once again had begun to transform. I began to blend in with my surroundings, which affected my physical movements as well as the mental connection I felt with my surroundings. I became more aware of the screaming insects and the movement within the trees as monkeys silently hopped from branch to branch along the treetops.

The river remained silent. Although I was near the river at this point, and I knew where it was, I rarely got a glimpse of it because of the thick wall of greenery growing out of the shallows of its banks. As I walked along the soft and slippery path, I noticed that there were many footprints, so I anticipated seeing someone at any moment.

I crept slowly out of my reverence for the jungle when I came to a small clearing along the riverbank. As I looked up, I saw a shirtless African with a string of medicine beads dangling loosely around his thin neck. He glided effortlessly with the flow of the river in his dugout canoe, paddling softly and unconsciously as he searched the bank with keen eyes, looking for signs of snapping turtles that he would feed to his family.

*He is beautiful,* I thought. *Thank God there still exists some pristine tradition left in the world.*

I cautiously moved into the open, waved my hand, and slightly bowed my head as a calm gesture. Upon seeing me, the charmed man excitedly waved his hand and stood up, exposing his sparking white teeth and his dark blue polyester slacks. My smile grew to match his, and he paddled to the shore.

He crashed to the shore and clumsily jumped out. His smile did not fade as he fought for control of his canoe, which the river was pushing downstream with great force. He had a very difficult time trying to avoid the influence that the river had on his handmade boat. If he moved the front of the canoe out towards the river, the current would catch its tip and yank on the worn rope, which he firmly held. If he pulled the front of the canoe toward the shore, a whirlpool would swing the boat farther into the swift river. It seemed that no matter what he tried to do, a force would act on the boat trying to drag it downriver and toward the city, Bangui.

I pondered whether I should help or not, and realized that by trying to help, I would only get in the way and make matters worse. After all, my being there was part of the reason this man was struggling.

No comprehensible words were exchanged between this man and me, but I understood that he wanted me to get into his boat with him.

"*Nous allons à ou?*" I asked, "Where would we go?" I asked, in hopes he understood French.

He then pointed to the bank across the wide river.

*That is Zaire*, I thought, wondering if this was a good idea. The issue wasn't about whether I could trust this man, but about what would happen if I got caught in Zaire without a visa. I pointed with my finger, moving it quickly to the opposite shore and back, trying to signify that I wanted to visit the Zaire side for only a very short time.

He excitedly bowed his head up and down.

The trip across the wide river and back was a bit more than I had expected. I became frightened at the power of the river. The African paddling the boat struggled constantly against the strong current. We were caught in a large whirlpool for a short time, but we made it across and back safely.

As I walked back toward Bangui, patches of areas cleared from logging and a more well-used dirt road became evident. I waved to two men walking toward their cassava field with machetes slung over their shoulders. A lone dog trotted by.

As I got to the outskirts of town, the road became lined with small huts often with hunted game hanging out front for people to purchase to feed their families. In front of one hut an elderly, shirtless woman pounded cassava. Three young children played with a small wire wheel, pushing it with a stick. The woman worked next to an old boom-box with one melted speaker. I could see the ribbon on the cassette tape spinning since the front cassette door was missing. The music was upbeat with a fast rhythm that wobbled a bit due to the age of the machine. The woman was smiling as she pounded the cassava. She invited me to sit with her.

I sat down on a small four-inch tall stool. She held out a betel nut for me, and I accepted it. Nodding my head to thank her, I looked at her weathered bare feet with thick strong skin, and I imagined all that this woman had seen during her long life living near the Ubangi River. We listened to the music as we sat next to each other, smiling.

## *About You*

*What was the best trip you've ever taken? Where was it? What's one interaction or moment that made the trip so wonderful?*

*In general, why do you think people travel? Do you think people usually get more, less, or something quite different from what they may have anticipated from traveling to another place?*

Do Something Extraordinary

*Think of a place you've always wanted to visit. Make a list of all the reasons you want to visit that particular place. Next make a list of things you'd need to do to make this trip a reality. Do at least one thing this week to work toward making your dream trip come true.*

# ELEVEN

# MORE THAN A BICYCLE RIDE

*West Coast, USA. 1987. Eighteen Years Old*

For years, when it came up, I'd tell people I rode my pedal-bike from Tacoma to Los Angeles, but this isn't entirely correct. Because I grew up in Tacoma and lived in LA, this just seemed easier to say. Actually the ride was from Olympia, Washington, to Santa Barbara in Southern California. Even so, it was still 1,200 miles along the winding Pacific Coast route.

I was seventeen when I asked my parents if I could do the ride. I don't think they would have let me go alone, but I was going to go with Tony, my high school Young Life leader, who was about six years older than me.

I had been riding a lot prior to this. I was hooked on bikes and spent as much time as possible on the road, pedaling as fast as I could to wherever I was going. I took long trips around Vashon Island, up to Seattle, and I'd even go to Redmond to race fixed-gear bikes on the velodrome once a week.

I was in love with my bike. It was a black and gold Shogun eighteen-speed. I paid for the bike by washing windows and mowing lawns, as well as with a little help from my great-grandmother. It wasn't an expensive bike, and by the time I ended up riding it down to California, it was a bit beat-up. It was equipped with a rotational spoke computerized odometer, water bottle holder, and emergency air pump.

As Tony and I prepared to leave, I also added a red handlebar bag and a homemade rear pannier rack since I couldn't afford a real one. I didn't have any brackets for the rack, so I just duct-taped it to the frame of my bike. It didn't look pretty, but it worked.

As soon as school got out for the summer, Tony and I planned to take off. Because Tony was in the Marine Corps Reserves, he ended up having a conflict of dates and couldn't do the entire trip. We decided that we would skip the area between Tacoma and Olympia, so my mom drove us down in our big red van, hugged us goodbye, and dropped us of at the interchange of I-5 and Highway 101 South.

Even though Tony and I hadn't ridden much together, we made a great team. We didn't talk much, and we made very good time. We'd draft back and forth. Within a few days we were out of Washington and into Oregon.

In the evenings, we'd stay at hiker-biker campgrounds, which were a dollar per night if a person was walking or on a bicycle.

Near the Oregon/California border, Tony had to return to report for duty. My high school friends, Shawn Fechter and Dave Lane, offered to drive down to pick up Tony. Since we were still young and didn't have wheels, they borrowed a car from another one of the Young Life leaders. I'm not exactly sure what they said they needed the car for, but I know that the car's owner was shocked when they returned it two days later and had clocked over a thousand miles on it.

I was sad to see Tony go. We'd become very close during that week riding together. His example of how a strong Christian man should act and treat people was very positive. He was also a great rider, and he helped push me to keep a very good pace.

It was a celebration when Shawn and Dave arrived. We met in the gravel parking lot of some motel along the 101. They loaded up Tony's bike, and we said goodbye.

As soon as they left, I felt strangely lonely. I walked over to a phone booth, called my parents, and told them that for the last half of the trip, I was on my own.

I started off a bit slower than normal, but as I warmed up, I began calculating to myself how much farther I had to go: about six hundred miles. I was halfway there, but I only had seven days to complete the ride because I was returning to Tacoma with Kris, my sister, who was going to Westmont College in Santa Barbara. Kris didn't have any flexibility on her departure date.

As I picked up the pace even more, I felt exhilarated. I rode a bit farther than my standard hundred-mile day and found a nice hiker-biker campground. At the campground, there were more cyclists than normal. There were about six tents around a communal fire pit.

I didn't plan for dinner very well on this day. All I had was a box of macaroni and cheese, but I had neither butter nor milk. I simply boiled the macaroni in my aluminum pot over the fire, poured out the water, and stirred in the powdery cheese.

The others at the fire looked at me curiously as I spooned the pasty, dry mac and cheese into my mouth. They were very nice. Unlike me, they all had fancy top-of-the-line bikes with nice canvas panniers on both the front and back. They were dressed in colorful, sleek Lycra, clip-in riding shoes, and aerodynamic helmets.

I sat there in riding shorts, but other than my skid-lid helmet, I really had no other special riding clothes. I simply wore a t-shirt, cotton socks, and tennis shoes. I did have black and gold fingerless riding gloves. I remember this because the shape of skimpy, fingerless gloves was suntanned onto my hands for months.

The next morning, I got up at about 7:30 and was on my bike by about 8:00. All the others were long gone. The serious riders had gotten up at six and left in no time at all. Even though I started later than them and my gear was not fancy like theirs—I was on a heavy bike with duct tape holding the racks on—by about 1 pm, I passed all of them. Not all at once, but within the span of about two hours, I passed them all. I tried not to be smug, just saying, "How's it going?" as I slid past. I couldn't help but wonder what they thought of my t-shirt and the duct tape in that moment.

I ended up seeing this group for three days in a row, and every evening they'd catch up arriving at the hiker-biker campsite well after me. They'd leave earlier in the morning, and I'd pass them usually just after 11 am.

On my third night alone, I wasn't close to any campgrounds, so after I had ridden as far as I could go, I entered a small town. I just put my tent up in the front yard of a small church. I really didn't see any other good options, and in the end, no one said a word, so I guess it was okay.

The riding was amazing. I think the thing I liked most was all the time alone I had with my thoughts. I thought about everything and sometimes nothing. At times, I was thinking deeply about the meaning of life, the universe, and everything. At other times, the theme song to Jeopardy would repeat in my head, without my permission, for hours. This song had my number, and I could do nothing about it. At times, other songs would get stuck in my head. Other times it really felt like a meditative nothingness, and I loved these times. Some moments I'd simply be in awe of my surroundings. I loved to see the different small communities, pastures, farms, woods, and beaches as I rode by.

I wasn't traveling at the pace of a car, but rather I was traveling at a pace in which I could feel my surroundings. I remember passing a giant pasture with many black and white spotted cows. I stopped to stare at them as I caught my breath. Probably because of the endorphins flooding my system from the strain of the ride, I felt like the cows and I had a divine connection.

At another point I was riding along miles and miles and miles of agricultural crops. The smell of lettuce, turnips, or whatever I was passing filled me. After hours, I became very hungry, but I had no food with me. I saw a head of lettuce on the side of the road that must have fallen off a truck. I stopped, peeled off the outer layer of leaves, and ate the whole thing right there. In that moment, surrounded by miles of lettuce and being very exhausted and starved, it tasted like the best food in the world.

That evening I found another hiker-biker campground, but the hiker-biker section was packed, so the park ranger told me that I could just use one of the normal campground spots for the same price. I selected a serene place just next to some trees. There were a few empty spots next to me toward the back of the campground. It was totally peaceful. I had the whole area to myself—for about forty-five minutes.

I was calmly cooking hotdogs when I began to hear the thunderous sound of many motorcycles approaching. I listened to them for minutes as they were idling near the park entrance. Then the sound multiplied as they came roaring into the campground. They immediately took over the three spots next to me. There were probably fifteen of them.

As they parked their radically customized Harleys, they get off and hugged each other jubilantly. It looked like they had had a long ride and were happy to get to their destination for the night. After a van pulled in and parked next to the bikes, it was swarmed as the men and women boisterously opened the back and pulled out ice chests full of beer and bottles of Jack Daniels. They began partying right away. Most pounded their first beer or took a shot of Jack from the bottle.

After a few minutes, two of the bikers noticed me. They began walking directly toward me. I looked back to see if there was something behind me, but no, they were coming toward me. My stomach tingled a bit as I sat still staring at the intimidating men approaching me. When they stopped right in front of me, the first guy asked, "Can I have one of your hotdogs?"

"Sure," I said and handed him a stick and an uncooked wiener. I was sitting on the ground near the fire. I tossed the bag of buns a few feet closer to him.

"Ha, ha," the gruff guy said to his friend with the smile of a kid. "This is gunna be good. I haven't had one of these in years." He stuck the hotdog on the stick and held it over the fire.

"Do you want one?" I asked the other bearded monster who, like all the others, was wearing a dirty vest with a big red, white, and yellow winged skull patch on the back.

"Yea, thanks," he growled.

I walked over and twisted a thin green branch off a bush a few feet away and handed it to him. With the large knife that was hanging from his belt, he sharpened the end of the branch. Both men were drinking beer, and it was as if we'd known each other for years. It was striking how with no introductions, they'd simply come over and made themselves at home.

Many years later, I would remember this episode when I was given a Harley-Davidson t-shirt. The front of the t-shirt had a beautiful scene of some bearded men riding motorcycles at night in the woods. Above the riders was a large full moon and a giant wolf in the sky looking over them. The text on the shirt said, "Legends Live Where Legends Roam."

The guys started asking about my ride, where I'd come from, where I was going. Once the group of bikers had created their own giant fire, I was invited over for a big feast of roasted tri-tip and pork that they'd been cooking. They were raucous, and I could tangibly feel the brotherhood that they shared. As they would play fight, hug, drink, and talk, everything was animated. That was the first day that I wanted to get a Harley-Davidson.

Even though the last wave of bikers didn't get to sleep until probably four in the morning, all of them were up and about when I got up at 7:30. I packed up my stuff and walked over to shake hands goodbye. One of the ladies, with long brown hair, hugged me to her black leather bikini and asked her old man if she could keep me. They all started cracking up, and I started blushing. I then thanked them for the feast the night before and started my long day of peddling. My thoughts that day on the bicycle consisted of dreams of getting my first motorcycle.

The next night I wanted to make it to San Francisco, or more precisely, San Mateo, where Dana, one of my mom's friends, lived. I was riding fast, and it didn't take too long to get to San Francisco. Riding over the Golden Gate Bridge was awesome, but it was freezing over the bay. The traffic slowed down a lot through San Francisco and along the busy streets down to San Mateo. In the end, I rode 140 miles that day and arrived very late. It was great to sleep in a bed, and I decided that I needed to take a day off, so I simply relaxed at their house the whole next day, listening to Dana's husband, who was a professional jockey, tell stories about his adventures racing horses. Then it was off to San Luis Obispo where I was going to see another one of my mom's friends.

You'd think riding south of San Francisco along Big Sur would have been one of the highlights of the trip, but it wasn't. Although I was riding along some of the most beautiful coastline cliffs in the world, it was a constant struggle of up and down along a narrow highway, and it was a bit windy. Gliding down the long and winding road was a nice reprieve but climbing back up from the low valleys was a challenge. I'd shift all the way down to first gear and simply put my head down and push up the steep corners and hills. Each pedal felt painful, my legs burned like they would explode, sweat was dripping off me wildly, and many times I wondered why I had done such a stupid thing as try to ride from Washington to California, but I kept struggling. I finally made it through, and the high I felt after the challenge made it all the more worth it.

It took me two days, and I was absolutely exhausted when I got to San Luis Obispo. I had been to Mary's house once before on a family vacation years earlier when I was about eight years old. That was when I realized the beauty of the California lifestyle. They had hammocks hanging between palm trees in their yard, shells along the edges of their garden, and surfboards leaning against the garage. The second day we were there, they went out and skin-dived for a few fish and abalone, which we ate for breakfast. We played in the sand and ocean waves. I loved it.

When I finally rolled up to Mary and Johnny's house, no one was home. I didn't want to ride another mile, so I just put my tent up in their back yard and put a note on their door that it was me back there. At about one in the morning, I heard Johnny fumbling with some keys. He called out, "Okay, got it, Erik."

I learned the following morning that Mary had been on the nightshift as a nurse at a hospital and Johnny, who was a professor, had been out with friends drinking beer and talking about math. In the morning, we had a lovely breakfast together, and then I was to start the last day of my ride.

The ride from San Luis Obispo to Santa Barbara is about a hundred miles, which is exactly how much I had been averaging. At this point my legs were toughened by the constant pedaling. They felt rock-solid.

After a huge breakfast, I pushed into the morning at a very quick pace. I was anxious to arrive. I was looking forward to seeing my sister, and I was also ready to be off the bike for a while.

I made that last stretch very quickly and was just entering Santa Barbara when I was suddenly overwhelmed with the feeling that I had to pee. It wasn't a gradual build up; rather, I had to go right now. I had peed while riding my bike during a half Ironman triathlon I had done earlier as well as a few other times while in small local races, so I knew what to do. I looked in all directions to make sure no one was around, and while coasting, I whipped it out and let her rip, angling down between my legs, so the wind wouldn't push the pee back onto me.

I was wrong that no one was around. While still in mid-piss, from behind I heard a loud voice on a speaker, which sounded like a megaphone. "Hold it right there!" the voice boomed emphatically.

Still peeing, I looked back to see a police car, with flashing lights, following right behind me.

I stopped, and the cop asked for my license. I handed him my Washington State driver's license.

He asked, "Is this what you guys do up in Washington?"

"Yes," I confirmed, "We do it all of the time. Kind of makes sense to pee in the middle of nowhere rather than peeing in your pants. What do you do here?"

It didn't go over very well. I had spent a total of nine dollars for "lodging," riding from Olympia to Santa Barbara, twelve hundred miles over fourteen days, and now this cop handed me a ticket for fifty-three dollars. I was pissed but took the ticket and pedaled on.

I was only a few miles from Kris's house when I'd gotten the ticket. As soon as I turned onto her street, my anger vanished. Kris knew I was coming, and she met me at the entrance to her neighborhood on a red moped. She did a U-turn next to me, and it was as if we were in a race with each other toward the finish. We smiled at each other.

I could see a large red ribbon strung across the front of her driveway, and a large sign that said, "Welcome Erik" and "Congratulations." There were also balloons tied to the mailbox. Of course, Kris, on her scooter, let me win.

As I ceremoniously rode through the red ribbon finish line totally fatigued from the ride, I felt great. I was smiling widely. I hugged Kris and began telling her about the ride, and as I did this, I realized that the ride was much more than I'd thought it would be.

Up in Washington, I simply loved to ride. I loved to put miles on my bike. During this trip, I felt the same, but it was also the landscapes and towns that I slowly passed, the terrific people I had met, and the time with my thoughts. Over all, it was simply about learning what the free feeling of being on the road meant, and I loved it.

## About You

*Have you ever set a lofty goal that others said was unreasonable? What was it and did you accomplish it?*

*How can setting goals add purpose to life? Is it possible that some people don't set goals because they secretly fear the work it might take to reach them or the disappointment they might feel if they don't accomplish the goal?*

Do Something Extraordinary

*Think of something you would like to do or accomplish, but which might not be very practical. Commit to making it a reality, and do at least one thing this week to move toward making it happen.*

## BONUS CHALLENGE

*Michael Gerber and others have shown that writing down goals increases the likelihood of the goals becoming a reality by a GIANT margin. I challenge you to take five minutes today and write down at least one short-term and one long-term goal you have. The next step that increases a goal's chance of happening is to read the goal to yourself every day until it is a reality.*

*If you are the type of person who loves challenges, go to www.ErikSeversen.com and check out the EXTRAORDINARY HABITS CHALLENGE. It's certain to help you become or continue to be extraordinary!*

# TWELVE

# BEHIND THE IRON CURTAIN

*Leningrad, USSR. 1989. Twenty Years Old*

It was 1987. I was a junior in high school. I was infatuated with the Soviet Union. It was near the apex of Mikhail Gorbachev's political shift of openness and the advent of his ideas of Glasnost and Perestroika. I closely followed as the relationship between Gorbachev and President Reagan developed. I also read every book in my high school library about Russian political leaders and history. I took a Russian language class at a community college. I wanted to somehow be connected to the historically important time I knew I was witnessing.

Also, I decided to go the USSR.

The only way I could get a visa to enter the totalitarian communist country was to join a guided tour. It took a bit of time to find a tour into Russia that I could afford since my only job was mowing lawns and washing windows. Finally, I found one that entailed entering Russia from Finland. It was 1989, and I was going to the USSR.

The trip from Helsinki to Leningrad was amazing. As we sped along in a train through the woods approaching the Russian border, I was excited to be entering behind the mysterious Iron Curtain.

When we got to the border, I felt anxious as all our passports were collected. Then the border police began calling people individually to be searched in one of the train cars that had been modified to look like an open clerk's office with green metal furniture. Although I had nothing to hide, the whole atmosphere was extremely tense. When my name was called, the guards became angry that I didn't stand up right away. I wasn't being defiant, but hearing the strong Russian accent, I didn't even recognize my name.

Finally, when I realized they were calling me, I gathered my large canvas backpack and, straining due to its weight, squeezed through the small door into the "search room" where I was asked to strip down to my boxer shorts and lay my belongings on the floor. All my items were noted on a declaration form in triplicate, and all my money was counted and documented as well. The stiff gentlemen in dark green and tan uniforms made it very clear that my belongings and money would be counted again in five days as I departed Russia. The statement felt like an ominous warning not to mess around with my declaration form.

I was in awe as we pulled into Leningrad (now called St. Petersburg). It looked just like the images in books I had read. There were some of the communist-built barracks-like buildings. Other buildings in the city were beautiful pastel colors along canals and small stone-arch bridges. Our tour group of about fifteen people stayed at a large state-run hotel. We were told that we could only shop at the state-run souvenir shops.

As an inherent explorer, I started to feel constricted by the confines set by our tour. After an afternoon ballet performance, I asked the young tour guide if I could explore away from the group. She said that as long as I checked in with her from time to time it would be fine. That was the last time, other than a few meals and an excursion to the Hermitage Art Museum, that I did anything with the tour group. I began to discover the city by myself.

It didn't take long before strolling down an ordinary street that I made my first friend. It was in the middle of the day, but the grayness made it feel almost dusk. A thin young man of about eighteen or twenty must have seen something different in me. He simply walked up and asked in a very heavy accent if I spoke English.

"Yes," I answered, and his smile grew immediately.

I had heard stories of Russian people wanting jeans, toothpaste, or anything they could get from the West, but this young man seemed to be content to just be near someone from the mysterious, capitalist USA.

We spoke for a very long time. His name was Vladimir. He told me that he had learned English by watching American movies. He asked if I wanted to visit his family's home. I told Vladimir that I'd meet him at the same place in the small brick plaza the following day.

"*Da Sveedahneea,*" I said waving goodbye and happy to use my first Russian word with Vladimir.

"*Da Sveedahneea,*" Vladimir said. "See you tomorrow," he added.

As I walked toward the plaza the following day, I felt nervous. I didn't think I was doing anything wrong, but I had an eerie impression that I was being watched. The day was again gray with a small drizzle of rain that didn't really make me wet, but mildly damp.

When I saw Vladimir from across the courtyard, he was smiling broadly and walking quickly toward me. He had gray trousers and an old brown overcoat that made him look exceptionally skinny. His greasy hair was brown and looked as if combed with his fingers. I thought I could trust Vladimir, but I really didn't know. I sensed that he was a good person, but I also sensed that there was something more to him than what I could identify.

After greeting each other with a hearty handshake, Vladimir seemed excited. I shivered a tiny bit in the cold as we turned to walk toward Vladimir's flat. He took my elbow in his hand as we walked. The walk to Vladimir's place took us off the main streets. The alleys became narrower. We ended up at a relatively tall block of cement buildings.

"This is it," Vladimir announced as he pushed through a heavy small door. We entered a small entryway with a tile floor and gated elevator. The elevator was tiny. I felt awkwardly close to Vladimir as he pushed the button to the seventh floor. We jerked upward. Through a narrow hallway, we stopped at an ornamented wooden door. Vladimir turned a key in the latch, and we entered the apartment.

Inside was very clean but cluttered with what seemed like generations of objects from lace doilies covering the backs of worn chairs, old glasses lined up neatly in glass-paneled hutches, and packed wardrobes that didn't shut all the way with clothes seemingly trying to push the doors open for air.

As soon as we stepped inside, Vladimir explained that his grandmother, parents, and sister lived in the flat, but no one was home. He then started showing me everything in the small room from small figurines and colorful Matryoshka dolls to old and new photographs on the wall to newspaper clippings about America. Obviously, Vladimir was as infatuated with the USA as I was with the Soviet Union.

After the tour of the small living room and tiny kitchen, Vladimir made tea. We sat for hours as he told me about his life in Leningrad and asked questions about my life back in the USA.

Vladimir showed me his collection of smuggled American movies, which were hidden in a trunk under a level of blankets and a level of Russian books. On a flickering TV set, we fast-forwarded through a few of the VHS movies as Vladimir asked me to explain a few phrases that he couldn't understand: "Enough is enough," "Pull my leg," and "Make my day."

As we spoke, Vladimir began describing a bit more about what his life was like and about the things that he did that probably were not approved of by strict Soviet regulations. He began to cautiously speak about the gray area of the rules and then in hushed tones about the necessity of the black market for survival.

I became slightly uncomfortable when I realized that Vladimir, maybe like many trying to make something more of themselves, saw me not only as a new friend and person with whom to practice English. He figured I might be someone who could possibly help him get through the next few weeks with a few more simple comforts beyond the basic substance afforded him by his parent's meager stipends. Vladimir didn't want my jeans, backpack, or jacket. He was too smart for that and knew that I would get in trouble if my declaration forms were incongruent when I left the USSR. What he wanted was to turn my United States dollars into Soviet rubles, and he knew people who could make it happen.

After probing me about the money I had already exchanged, I truthfully told Vladimir that through the tourist exchange at the hotel, I got four rubles to one US dollar.

As soon as I told him this, his eyes got wide. He informed me, "I can get you forty per dollar."

I asked all the questions I could think of that would allow me to do it without getting in trouble. Vladimir was upfront that he'd get a bit of the cut from the man who would do the exchange. We discussed that as long as I didn't purchase any physical objects to leave the country with, my declaration forms would stay consistent. Also, his friend had copies of official exchange receipts that would show that I received "in fact" four rubles to the US dollar. As long as I spent four of the forty rubles from each dollar at a state-run shop, all would be fine.

Looking Vladimir in the eye and reading him as well as I could, with nervousness I asked, "Can I trust you?"

Vladimir didn't blink as he replied, "*Da*."

I did trust him. We made an appointment to have coffee with his contact for 9:00 pm that same evening.

As soon as the appointment was set, I was filled with anxiety, an anxiety over questions about doing the right thing as well as a fear of being caught. I thought of Raskolnikov from Dostoyevsky's *Crime and Punishment* and of his own mental anguish over executing a crime for what he thought was a good reason. The distinction that Raskolnikov was pondering murder while I was considering exchanging a few dollars for rubles didn't register. Even if it had, it wouldn't have alleviated any of my anxiety.

As we waited in Vladimir's tiny, dark flat, time moved slowly. I imagined Raskolnikov sitting in his own tiny St. Petersburg room pondering his would-be illicit actions, and I felt like I understood Dostoyevsky in a way I had missed before. I felt like *Crime and Punishment* wasn't as much about a murder plot as it was about the condition of nervousness, a nervousness that was present in Vladimir's daily life. When I mentioned my anxiety to Vladimir, he calmly stated that one either accepts shortage or endures the anxiety while attempting to create a better condition.

Once we arrived at the cafe, I was introduced to Vladimir's contact. We ordered vodka and chatted. I felt privileged to be in the lively scene. We spoke about philosophy and poetry and the ballet I had seen the prior day. As casually as we could, the agreed upon currency was exchanged with clandestine hands under the small square table. Everything worked out exactly as Vladimir had planned. By Russian standards, I suddenly had a lot of money in my pocket.

The first thing I did the following morning was take a two-hour taxi tour of Leningrad. With phrasebook and map in hand, I basically had the taxi driver show me everything he thought was interesting in the city. I ate at nice restaurants. I invited a man from the tour and his family to dinner. After a number of vodka shots, I let him know about the black-market exchange I was getting. He couldn't keep it quiet. The result was that over the next few days, other people from the tour gave me USD asking if I'd exchange it for them. I was happy to do it.

Having the extra money was exciting since it was so different from my standard method of frugal travel, eating little, and sleeping in low-end hostels or even on park benches. However, without being able to purchase anything I could take with me, it was difficult to spend what I had. As I found myself on a train headed for the Finland border, I suddenly was struck with a pit in my stomach. *Oh, no, I* thought to myself. *I've still got a pocketful of Russian rubles.*

We still had a long way to go to the border, and most passengers would get off before it. As the train wheels clanked along the track, I slowly stood up and scanned all the faces of the people sitting on the train as I walked three cars down toward a restroom. I would have loved to have chosen who to give the money to on the train, but I couldn't risk someone informing the Russian police.

After entering the bathroom, I sat on the lid of the toilet for a moment, thinking. Then I reached into my right front jeans pocket and pulled out an inch-and-a-half wide roll of colorful rubles held together with a thin rubber band. I looked at it wondering how much was there. I slowly placed the cylinder upright in the center of the lime-green floor of the tiny bathroom, an anonymous gift to the next person who would enter.

## *About You*

*Have you ever met someone whose circumstance was so totally different from yours that you wondered what it would be like to live their life? Who was it and what was their circumstance?*

*Is it easier to find purpose in life with or without many comforts and material possessions? How do material comforts affect a person's pursuit of purpose in life?*

*Do Something Extraordinary*

*Think through your material possessions and choose one thing, maybe a nice book or jacket, and give it away. Even better, go through your possessions and give away everything you haven't used or worn in over a year.*

# THIRTEEN

# MUAY THAI

*Bangkok, Thailand. 1997. Twenty-Seven Years Old*

It took a minibus, water taxi, tuk tuk, and short walk down an alley to get to the Muay Thai camp and kickboxing school, but I made it. It was in a crowded neighborhood near Thon Buri in Bangkok.

Once I found it, I discovered it was composed of a large cement area beneath a house on wooden stilts. A few faded heavy bags hung from rafters, and there were pads and equipment stacked in the area as well. The centerpiece was a raised full-sized boxing ring with blue canvas and red, white, and blue ropes.

The place was abuzz with sound and movement as many boys and young men, all in colorful Muay Thai boxing shorts, were training with great intensity, either individually or in pairs. The din of the many guys pounding on bags, pads, and each other was powerful. Some were stretching, some jumping rope, some shadow boxing, and others were punching, kicking, and elbowing each other.

No one stopped training when I approached, but most glanced at me with curiosity, momentarily distracted from what they were doing. It was a hot and humid day, as usual, and all were breathing hard and dripping with sweat.

I stood in the alley, which was also being used by some boxers, and watched the display. Then I noticed a mostly exposed plywood shower with a cement floor and a closet-sized office underneath large wooden steps leading to the house above.

Approaching the small office, I came upon a lean, fit, and dark-skinned man looking through some scraps of paper. He stood up, and I placed my palms together in front of my chest in a Thai bow and greeting, known as *wai*. He did the same to me. Next, I greeted him with the Thai *"Sawatdee krup,"* and then said that I wanted to train at the camp.

In extremely broken English, the man informed me that it wasn't possible because it was a camp for Thai boxers. Also, the coach didn't speak English.

Since this was only a few years after the first UFC fight, and martial arts tourism did not really exist yet, I'd expected this.

"I understand," I replied. Next, I produced a letter of introduction that I had gotten from a Thai Temple in Federal Way, Washington, back in the USA. Pang, a Thai friend of mine, had taken me to the temple to explain to the monk that I wanted to go to Thailand to train Muay Thai. Pang explained that I had already been training in the USA for a number of years and that I wanted to learn from the source. The monk spent over an hour talking with us. He was very jovial and went back and forth, speaking Thai with Pang and English with me.

Before arriving at the temple, Pang explained that there were a few protocols that I should respect. First, while sitting with the monk, I should keep my head lower than his. I should sit on my knees with my feet straight behind me and never pointing in his direction. This wouldn't seem difficult, but the monk, with his shaved head and full-length bright orange sarong, was quite a bit shorter than me. Even though he was sitting cross-legged on a three-inch platform in front of me, I felt awkward trying to squish my body down on my legs to stay low enough.

We sat like this for over an hour until the monk wanted to show me something on the Thailand map that hung on the wall. As I tried to stand up, my legs were totally and utterly asleep. I was like a new-born fawn trying to stand for the first time. I almost fell into a gold tree with clips of offered dollar bills hanging from it.

Luckily the monk and Pang were ahead of me as we crossed the room, so they didn't see this wild wobbling. As soon as we reached the map, I grabbed the wall to hold myself up.

With the blood starting to flow back into my legs, I was able to direct my attention to the monk who was pointing his finger at Bangkok on the map. Once he said I should go there, an evident excitement began to grow in me. I realized, for the first time, that I might really be going to Southeast Asia to box. At the end of the wonderful time with the monk, he gave me the name of a Muay Thai camp that was run by someone he had grown up with in Thailand.

He scripted a simple letter of introduction in Thai and made it official with a small wax seal from his temple.

I handed the introduction letter to the man at the camp who had introduced himself as Po. He read the letter and looked up at me like he didn't know what to do. It was clear that he didn't really want me to be there distracting the fighters, but he said that I should go home and return the next day. In the meantime, he would show the letter to *Ajarn* Chatit. I knew by the title of *Ajarn* that Chatit was the founder of the camp, and I assumed correctly that Po was *Kru* or teacher.

The following day, I arrived with my boxing gear. The scene at the outdoor gym was the same as the day before except that Po walked toward me right away and led me into the tiny office to introduce me to *Ajarn* Chatit. After greeting each other with the *wai,* Chatit began speaking to Po who translated as best he could. Chatit explained through Po that I could train at the camp, but that if I decided not to return the following day, there would be *"mai pen rai"* or "no problem."

Po quickly showed me where to place my bag and pointed that I should put on my boxing shorts in the tiny shower. With almost no English, but a lot of charades and body gestures, he told me to warm up, stretch, and kick one of the wooden pillars, which were wrapped in battered hemp rope, 200 times. Then I should let him know when I was finished.

Once finished, I was exhausted. My shins ached from kicking the solid pole over and over. I picked up my already soaking wet towel and tried to wipe the sweat from my face and body.

I limped over to Po, trying not to show my fatigue, and he gestured that I should jump rope. The bottoms of my bare feet were already getting raw from working out on the cement. Blisters had begun developing, but I started jumping rope.

After about ten minutes, Po returned with a set of red Thai kicking pads that he strapped to each of his forearms. I knew the drill: he would move the pads either to the left or right as a signal for me to round kick as quickly and powerfully as I could; or he would hold the pads vertically for me to punch or elbow; or angled down and crossed for me to knee with all my might. After only minutes of this, I was becoming light-headed, but we continued.

Finally Chatit came over. He had been working with guys in the center ring, and now it was my time. I was asked to put on my full boxing gloves, rather than bag gloves, and was told to enter the ring over the ropes, not through them.

Once in the ring, Chatit also had Thai pads on his forearms as well as open-fingered padded gloves covering his knuckles. After a respectful *wai*, we began much the same way that I had with Po. Quickly the pace increased. None of the other fighters stopped training, but all eyes were curious about what was happening in the center ring with the foreign newcomer.

As the pace quickened, Chatit also began kicking and punching me. Po yelled that I could hit him back. As the aggressiveness continued to mount, Chatit roughly grabbed the back of my neck a few times and closed the distance between us, offering that I could clinch when I wanted. I should add that Chatit had also been working for a long time with others in the ring, but he didn't seem tired while I was gasping for air.

Although he was becoming very aggressive, kicking me as well as defending my kicks, Chatit was smiling. There was nothing mean about what he was doing, but he definitely wanted me to know what I was getting into. I began to understand what Po meant when he warned that if I didn't want to show up again, they would understand.

Then it really began to happen. I heard Chatit speak English for the very first time. "USA!" he shouted as he did a straight front kick to my stomach. The extremely fast kick sent me flying back into the ropes and down to the canvas.

I was stunned. I rose as quickly as I could, pushing my body off the blue mat and leaving a wet body print below me. Chatit was still moving; it wasn't over. He allowed me plenty of time to get up and even get oriented before he came at me. "USA!" he yelled again as he punched me squarely on the chin.

Sweat shot from my hair, and I buckled again, hitting the mat. Wobbly, I rose.

Chatit, like a cat playing with a mouse and enjoying himself, let me get into a rhythm, which was becoming more impossible as I also fought the fatigue that was overcoming me. Chatit kicked, punched, and kneed me at will. Because he was holding himself back, they were not powerful blows, but they continued. My head already hurt and my ears were ringing.

Then came the finale also accompanied by the shout, "USA!" With no possibility of protecting myself from this fifty-year-old master fighter, he did a classic Muay Thai round kick to my floating ribs, instantly knocking the wind out of me and flinging me once again to the canvas.

Immediately Chatit slid off his gloves and pulled on my drenched forearms to help me up. Once I was standing, we both ended the session with the respectful *wai*, placing our palms together in prayer position just below our chins and bowing our heads slightly. I was still heaving but smiled as much as I could. After I got out of the ring, Po congratulated me, but I could tell he didn't think I'd be back.

On the way back to my apartment I was still wobbling. I even had a difficult time jumping from the long, thin klong river boat taxi. The small hop was only 2.5 feet, but I barely made it out of the bobbing boat and onto the wooden dock without falling into the murky water. As I walked past the small gang of motorcycle taxi drivers at the corner of the alley where I was living, they smiled at how I looked, nodding and chuckling as I past them.

The next day, I was extremely sore, but I went back to the camp. I was tortured in much the same way. It was a few weeks of this before I had begun to gain some respect at the Muay Thai camp. The respect wasn't for my skills as much as my willingness to continue getting up each time I was knocked down.

When I began sparring, Chatit and Po had me spar with guys close to my weight. It was like a car wreck. Then they had me spar with much smaller guys. Although the kicks and punches never really hurt, my opponents were so quick that they could land ten for every one of mine. I wasn't able to get any really powerful shots on them.

One day, Po told me that there was a guy visiting the camp who spoke English. He wanted me to spar with him. During the sparring session, I felt great at how well I had done against this very good opponent. I was bleeding but felt like I had really stuck with him. It was a pretty even match.

After the fight, I approached they guy, eager to have suggestions in English. I said to him, "Thanks for that. Hey, just so I can continue to get better, was there anything you saw that would help me improve?"

He answered, "Yes, you know when I kicked you there?" and he pointed to the outside of my thigh at my femur. He had kicked me there very hard about six times.

"Yes," I said.

"You have to block that," he explained, "I could have broken your leg on all of those."

"Oh," I replied, feeling humbled but thankful that he had shared this. I was also thankful that he hadn't broken my leg. We both smiled and parted with a *wai*.

After a few months at the camp, the time arrived. Po said that he wanted me to fight a guy at Bangkok University named Aawut. I learned that Aawut was a relatively new, but good fighter who had even fought at Lumpini, the most famous Muay Thai arena in Thailand. I realized that although Po kept using the term "sparring," this was being talked about like it was a big event though there would be few spectators. The date for the fight was three weeks into the future.

Nervousness for the fight immediately began to creep inside me. I knew it was a big deal when Po said that Chatit wanted to teach me the *wai kru* from his camp.

The *wai kru* is the certain ceremonial bow performed before a fight. It moves directly into the *ram muay*, which is a ritualized dance. The *wai kru* starts from the sitting-on-knees position and is made up of three elaborate bows with the arms making a large, wide circle. It ends with the hands on the floor usually with a triangle made by index finger and thumbs and the forehead touching the tips of fingers on the floor, as much as it can over the boxing gloves. This is done generally three times to represent respect to God, family, and the Muay Thai teacher.

Next is the *ram muay*, a rhythmic show of flexibility, dexterity, and ferocity with artistic movements mimicking winning over an opponent and sometimes even shooting an imaginary bow and arrow at them. I knew that if Chatit and Po wanted me to perform these before the fight, they took it seriously.

Although standard Muay Thai fights are five rounds, this exhibition was to be three rounds of three minutes each. Knowing how much energy even three rounds would take, I immediately began to take my training to a new seriousness. My training became more consistent and focused. A few days before the fight, Po said that he wanted me to make an offering to Buddha at Wat Po, a very special temple in Thailand not far from the camp. He suggested that I put a gold flake on the Buddha statue.

This sounded simple enough to me. I had seen it done. Basically, a person just buys a small square sheet of plastic, which has a small, less-than-paper-thin wafer of gold on it.

The idea is to put the gold side on the statue and slide the plastic off of it, leaving the offering of a tiny leaf of gold clinging to the Buddha.

Upon entering the majestic temple compound, I gazed up at the white buildings with their steep red roofs and orange and golden spires with detailed gold flames reaching into the sky. Wat Po is known for its giant reclining Buddha, but I sought out a more modest statue in a building surrounded by blue demon-like gargoyles.

I was with Thong, a new Thai friend, and he walked me through the process of offering the gold to the Buddha. Even with Thong's careful instruction, I hit a snag. While trying to slide the flake of gold from under the plastic, my fingers came in contact with the many flakes of gold that were already stuck on the Buddha. The thin flakes from the Buddha immediately clung to my moist fingers. I tried to fix it by tapping the flakes down to get them to stick back onto the Buddha, but everything I did made it worse.

I looked at Thong for help, but he didn't know whether to laugh or be frightened. It was supposed to be a very serious moment, but it was going horribly wrong—instead of offering a flake of gold to the Buddha, I was taking flakes from the Buddha—and that was what was so funny about it. The harder I tried, the worse it became. I suddenly had gold covering all the fingers on my right hand and a few on my left as I tried to assist with it as well. Finally, I looked around to see if anyone was watching and tried to shake and rub the gold off my fingers. Indeed, I had taken way more gold off the Buddha than I had placed on it.

I decided that getting a magical tattoo called a *yun* would be a much easier way to gain protection during the fight. My *yun* ended up between my shoulder blades at the bottom of the back of my neck. My *yun* was tattooed with a bamboo splinter and black ink. It was scripted by a monk who created a spire in the middle, and the writing in Thai below it read, *"Praja, Santipup, Lak,"* which means "God, Calm, Love." Although I wasn't convinced that it would help protect me from getting injured while kickboxing, I did enjoy what the monk had selected to put on me.

As I had been living in Sukumvit and training in Thon Buri, I began get to know the people along my route to and from the training camp. My apartment was on the corner of Sukumvit Road and an alley called Soi 13 or *Soi Sibsam*. On that corner, there was a small motorcycle gang with radically customized tiny 125cc sport bikes. These guys were also the local cut-through-lanes taxi service for the area.

Since I passed them every day, we became quite familiar with each other. They often offered me a glass of beer or whiskey as I passed, and we'd sit on the curb and chat for a bit. After a particularly brutal day at the camp, I passed much later than normal, and they were well into their Mekong whiskey. As they often did, they offered me one, and I sat down.

After one whiskey turned to four, one of the guys suddenly decided he wanted to slap box. Prodded on by his friends, the young man, still wearing his colorful blue and yellow silk "motorcycle vest" over his shirt, put his hands up and began the rocking back-and-forth motion, with his hands held wide in front of his face in the traditional Thai boxing stance.

A bit buzzed myself and excited to test my speed against him, I stood up and joined the dance. It started as if we were two cobras swaying back and forth at the start of a duel. We quickly began tapping each other with open fingers and kicking quickly but lightly at each other's legs. I was proud that I was winning. I began to smile widely as it became evident that I was beating him. That was where the fun ended.

Hating the fact that a *farang* or Westerner was beating him at his national sport of kickboxing, the pace increased rapidly until the real punch came. He hit me square in the face as hard as he could. I punched him back hard and as I went into a clinch, he elbowed me rapidly four times with the tips of his elbows striking the sides of my forehead. I kneed him and punched wildly as hard as I could as he was doing to me. It was a frantic mess of a fight. Happily, the rest of the crew broke up the fight almost as quickly as it had started, but both of us were a mess.

Blood poured from my opponent's nose, and I didn't know it yet, but I had cartoon-like massive bumps on each side of my forehead that looked like bright red horns. As soon as we were pulled apart everyone was yelling at both of us to make up, so we shook hands as well as *wai'*-ed each other and then laughed at what had happened.

Once the quick jolt of anger was gone, we poured another whiskey, laughing at each other's injuries. There was a curious closeness that developed in our friendship after that. I was gaining a respect amongst the locals because of my dedication to training in their sport, and there was one moment when this respect saved me.

Several times I visited a nightclub called Four Kings in Pat Pong, the most notorious red-light district in Bangkok. Since there was a girl I liked back in the USA, I wasn't into picking up girls, but I did love to go out on Saturday nights and dance into the wee hours of the morning, fueled on mass quantities of Red Bull and amphetamines. On one evening, it was still only just after midnight, and a cute Thai girl from about ten feet away mirrored my dancing for a few seconds. We smiled at each other and that was it. Then, a very muscular but quite short white guy with short hair came up to me and shouted, "Not with her!"

"What?" I asked, confused and wondering what this dude was trying to do.

"She's with him," he stated as he pointed to a very large and strong-looking guy from India. "Stay away from her," he ordered.

We were still in the middle of the dance floor, people dancing all around us, and the music was loud. I walked over to the Indian guy next to the girl, leaned in towards his ear, and said, "Listen, man. I'm not looking for a fight, and I'm not looking to pick up a girl. You look cool." As I said this, I grabbed his hand and gave him a thumbs-up fist handshake. Then I turned to the white guy again and asked, "Now, who the fuck are you?"

He yelled that the Thai girl was with the Indian guy and that I should leave. I could see in his eyes that he was very worked up and was ready to fight. In another similar situation, a few years earlier with a bouncer at a bowling alley, I hadn't known it was a fighting situation, and I was head-butted in the face, unprepared. Since then I promised myself that I'd never get caught off-guard again, so I decided to find out.

"Do you want to fight?" I yelled just so I knew what was about to happen.

"We all do" was the response from one of the other three white guys who were now standing next to him. The standoff between me and four other foreigners had now cleared a wide circle in the middle of the dance floor as people got out of the away. As I pondered what to do, I knew it was going to be messy, but I held my position firm with no intention of leaving.

Suddenly, the look on all four of the guys' faces changed into what looked like confusion or fear as six Thai guys entered the clearing and stood calmly beside me with three on each side of me. They didn't look aggressive, but their intimidation was as evident as if I had pulled a gun. Without a word, the four white guys simply turned and walked out of the club.

I wai'-ed each of the young Thai men who were standing next to me, individually placing my palms together in front of my chin and looking at each of them in the eye. They each gave a small smile knowing how much I appreciated how they had saved me, and then they walked back to the tables they had come from at the edges of the dance floor without a word.

It took me some time to find the two friends I had come to the club with. Many people were talking with them.

"Did you see that?" I asked.

"We heard about it," one of them said with a large smile.

"What happened? Why did the Thai guys do that?" I asked.

"Evidently, you're known here," Thong said. "You're known as the crazy white guy who isn't looking for Thai women and who likes to blow his brains out on chemicals on Saturday nights. They also know you train Muay Thai."

"Wow," I said.

"The guys who stood next to you know of you from boxing," Thong continued. "They wouldn't let anything bad happen to you."

I immediately felt fraternal with the guys who came to my side. When they did this, I felt like the most powerful person in the room. I wanted to thank each of them again, but I had already done that. I felt honored, but the gift of their alliance also humbled me. Throughout the rest of the hours, as night turned to early morning, many people smiled at me as I danced by myself, and others patted me on the back as they walked by. I think all who had witnessed the standoff were proud of the guys who had come to my aid. I, the "local" *farang* was safe, and they were now local heroes.

When I entered my Muay Thai camp two days after the incident, a few of the guys I had been training with excitedly mentioned that they heard what had happened at the club. Then it was back to it. I had a lot of work to do to prepare for my upcoming match.

The day before the match, I was already numb with nerves. As I walked down an alley off Sukumvit Road I didn't notice the many smells and colors that I normally experienced as I passed people selling clothes, handbags, grilled snacks, spices, and other things along the narrow, uneven sidewalk. As if in a tunnel, I walked and sat on the tiny metal stool at the small metal table at the noodle cart where I often ate. The cups of herbs and spices and jars of spoons and chopsticks on the table were invisible to me.

As I sat down, the woman at the noodle stand asked, *"Tom Krueng Nai?"* She knew that this was my most common meal from her.

*"Krab,"* I responded, meaning yes, she was correct.

Although I knew it took her a bit of time to wet the noodles before placing the various organs and meat into the steaming bowl, it seemed like it was instantly in front of me, but I could barely eat. After playing with the soup for a few minutes, the woman at the stand looked at me concerned. We often joked without sharing more than a few common words, but she could tell I wasn't in a joking mood. She just looked at me with a worried, wrinkled brow. I felt warmed by her. She had a blue and white bandana around her head with a wet strand of black hair hanging in front of her worried face. I tried to smile, and I said, "I'm okay," in English, but I knew she didn't understand. I knew that I had no words in Thai to let her know that I was simply nervous about a boxing match and that everything was really okay. I finally got the soup down only because I knew I'd need the energy. I paid the forty baht for the meal and went back to my place.

When I met Chatit and Po before the fight, they looked calm. Normally, I always wrapped my own hands with my hand wraps, but Po insisted on doing it this time. Then Chatit gave me a red *mongkul*, which is a tightly wound, stiff headband that stuck out from behind the head by a few inches with silk tassels on the end. The *mongkul* they gave me was red with blue and white tassels hanging off the ends at the back. As Chatit held the *mongkul* in his hands, I gave him a more emphatic than normal *wai*. He placed it on my head and *wai'*-ed me in return. Po smiled broadly.

There really weren't a lot of people watching the many fights taking place. When it was time for me to go, Chatit, Po, and a few others from the camp walked with me to the red corner of the ring. I had on red boxing shorts that said, over the front of the shorts, "Muay Thai," in Thai script in blue letters with white outlines.

As always, when I entered the ring, I jumped over the top rope. Po instructed me to walk around the entire ring right at the start with my hand sliding along the top rope as a way of defining my space and owning the ring. He even said that if my opponent was to be standing near the ropes, so I couldn't pass, that I should stand politely as long as it took for him to step away, so that I could continue the circuit of the ropes. When I got back to my corner, Po adjusted my *mongkul* and gestured that I should begin my *wai kru ram muay*.

Since the *wai kru ram muay* is a very important part of a Muay Thai camp, I felt as anxious about doing it as I did about the actual fight. Once I started, I felt calm, especially during the third bow with my forehead pressed to my gloves on the floor in front of me as I silently ran though the names of all the people who had trained me, both back in the USA and ending with Po and Ajarn Chatit who were with me. When I finished the respectful and elaborate three-tiered bows and the slow, rhythmic combative dance, I walked back to my corner to watch my opponent perform his.

My nerves returned ten-fold, but Aawut looked relaxed. His tan, cut muscles looked sharp. He had blue shorts, a yellow *mongkul*, and gold cloth armbands called *prajioud* wrapped above his biceps with short tassels hanging off them. Aawut never took his eyes off mine during his display. Indeed, Aawut's *ram muay* intimidated me.

The first round was a dog fight and was actually quite even. It was much faster paced than most of the other fights. Although most of the world had disappeared, I was aware of the excited scream of *"Oiy"* from the spectators every time one of us kneed the other. In the middle of the second round, however, I began to breathe too hard. More and more of the world outside of the ring began to come back. I began thinking too much, and exhaustion was slowing my movements.

It was evident that my opponent was beating me, but I continued. I pushed deep. Near the end of the third round, I was becoming totally gassed out and light-headed. I was suffocating and thought about the dangerous position I was now getting myself into without being able to defend myself adequately. I knew that one perfect kick from the lower shin of my opponent to my face or head would surely send me to the hospital; or he could break my femur, which was less concerning, but a possibility.

I was sweating hard, and it felt like my pores were stinging. I sucked air trying to keep my teeth closed over my mouthpiece while at the same time getting all the precious oxygen that I could. Dizzy, I thought about giving up. Then I heard in English from somewhere, "Only thirty seconds left." Neither I nor my opponent had been knocked down during the entire fight, and I didn't want it to happen. I wanted to last the entire match. *How bad can he hurt me in thirty seconds?* I thought to myself, motivating myself.

My only goal in those thirty seconds was not to go down, and Aawut sensed it. He wanted the total opposite of what I wanted, and he attacked with everything he had. He hit, kicked, and then grabbed the back of my neck, clinching my neck with his forearms, swinging me around from side to side, kneeing me in the stomach, twisting me, and doing the same to my kidneys. He tried to kick my legs out from under me. The wind was knocked out of me many seconds before the end of the fight.

I had one goal: not to go down. I almost passed out, but I didn't.

*I won*, I said to myself emphatically and proudly as the final bell rang. *I did it,* I said again to myself.

Immediately, I tried to stand up straight but remained in a hunched over position trying to get my breath back. The referee pointed to the corner I was supposed to return to, and I'm glad he did because I'm not sure I could have found it if he hadn't. I could only hobble. I couldn't even recognize the red from the blue corner, let alone the fussy faces of Chatit and Po who stood in my corner.

They put their hands up with arms wide as if guiding an airplane to land, but they were only guiding me to them in the corner. They weren't cheering, but they didn't look disappointed. They both hugged me.

I wanted to vomit from the exhaustion as well as from the simple shock my body had gone through. My eyes were not completely adjusted yet, but the referee immediately wanted us to return to the center of the ring. The judges needed no time in figuring out who had won.

By the time the referee raised Aawut's arm in victory, at least my mind was mostly back to normal, even if I was still ill with fatigue.

Aawut stepped in front of the ref and hugged me. He said in very broken English something like, "I thought you go down. I thought you knock out. You good boxer."

I felt honored, but I also thought this was hilarious since other than maybe part of the first round, he had dominated the fight. We both knew that I had won in my own little way by refusing to go to the mat, so he grabbed my arm and raised it up.

The small crowd all wanted Aawut to win mostly because he was Thai, but they cheered vigorously when Aawut raised my arm to share the victory. I felt a lump grow in my throat and had to fight to keep tears from forming in my reddening eyes.

Aawut then actually walked me back into my corner, a motherly and protective gesture, making sure I was okay. At this point I was, and as I turned around to *wai* him, I felt a sense of love. We had each done as much as we could to hurt and even injure the other in the ring within the bounds of the rules, but the moment it was over, I felt like Aawut would do anything to protect me. I would have done the same for him. We had tested each other and battled, and now it was over. We were two brothers who understood each other in ways almost impossible in any place outside of war or the ring.

The day after the fight, my body was a wreck. My eyes were swollen. My legs were so sore that I could barely walk straight, but I felt high from the experience. Part of me never wanted to box again because of the pain, and part of me wanted to go to the Muay Thai camp and try to train that very day. Instead, I hobbled down to my standard noodle stand seeing many people I recognized.

I felt alive due to the sights and sounds of the many small motorcycles, blue and yellow tuk tuks, colorful clothes for sale, and strings of yellow flowers and incense on the small alters in front of almost every tiny storefront. The colors and smells filled me as I walked past the heat of the steaming water in the noodle cart. I sat on the hot metal bench at the hot metal table under the shade of a bedsheet that had been converted into an awning. I felt privileged to be there, and it showed on my beat-up face.

The woman who worked the noodle stand saw me sit down. Immediately she came over and sat next to me. Even though I looked beat up, she no longer seemed worried, but rather excited. She could tell I was at peace. She had the same blue and white bandana tied around her head. Her hair was still hanging down in front of her face, but her worried look was gone. She began speaking to me in Thai. Although I had no idea what she was saying, I smiled and made little boxing motions with my hands to confirm that I was in a Muay Thai match.

She said something else in Thai, and for some reason, I thought the answer deserved a yes. As I always did when she guessed correctly which soup I would have, I said, "Krab." She then stood up and excitedly said something to all the others sitting at the four tiny tables and to the people sitting on the steps of the small neighboring shops. They all cheered in unison, and many of them put their arms up with an encouraging sign of victorious congratulations. I then realized that I had answered yes to the question whether I won the fight or not. I knew it would be useless to try to correct the mistake, so I simply smiled and accepted the praise since in my mind I really had won something.

For years, I'd been telling myself that I wanted to come to Thailand to learn Muay Thai from the source. Even though I never won a single match in Thailand, except for the one against the motorcycle taxi guy, I had indeed learned from the source. And I learned that the source is the best. Also, I learned that it was about much more than just the boxing.

## *About You*

*Have you ever really wanted to accomplish something and when you did, you realized that something else resulted from the accomplishment that was even more meaningful to you? What was the accomplishment and what was the meaningful by-product?*

*What are some of the main reasons that some people do not pursue goals?*

*Do Something Extraordinary*

*Think of your three biggest goals and ask yourself what positive, non-direct results can come from striving for and reaching them. Write your goals down and take action this week toward one of them.*

# FOURTEEN

## CHALLENGE OF THE MOUNTAIN

*Washington State, USA. 2015. Forty-Six Years Old*

Hunched over under the weight of a forty-pound backpack, on a steep angle of ice and leaning into the wind, I took another laborious step forward. Based on the time, which was about five in the morning, and visualizing the weather forecast we'd studied the prior morning, I estimated that the wind had reached about sixty-five miles per hour, but it felt like a hurricane. Plus, I'd only slept for about an hour the previous night. I struggled with each small step, knowing that each would take me a few inches closer to the summit.

Even through the goggles, I had to squint due to the force of the wind. The sting of blown snow whipped my face in the small gaps between my orange climbing helmet and down jacket. We were on a very narrow ledge with a massive crevasse looming below us. We were at the upper part of Ingram Glacier on Mt. Rainier. I was roped to Carl, Glen, and Andrew, three friends who were behind me. If one of us slipped, it would be up to the other three to dig in with crampons and ice axes in an attempt to arrest the fall.

It wasn't our first time attempting this mountain. We desperately wanted to beat the storm to the summit. But, as conditions worsened, Andrew, at the lower end of the rope, decided it was beyond his level of calculated risk, so he refused to continue.

"What is wrong?" I shouted as loudly as I could into the wind toward Carl who was behind me on the fifty-meter rope. He was calling back, but I couldn't hear anything. As I fought to keep my balance, I motioned for the others to come up to me. They shook their heads no. Finally, I had to climb down to them.

Andrew informed us that he wasn't going to go another step up the mountain. Against the pressure of the wind, he screamed that he thought we'd be blown off the glacier or die in the storm if we continued. I seriously wanted to continue and so did Carl. Andrew dug in firm that he was not continuing, and we couldn't split up in such inclement weather.

"We're almost there!" I exclaimed through the wind just as my sleeping pad was ripped from my backpack in the violent gale and flew horizontally away from us and down into a distant crevasse below. At that, I realized that once again, the mountain wasn't going to let us reach her peak.

Furious, I turned around. We fought our way down to Camp Muir. A mixture of sand, rocks, and snow blasted us as we descended Disappointment Cleaver and crossed Cathedral Gap. The normally mild hike down Muir Snowfield to Paradise also proved a challenge as whiteout conditions increased the closer we got to the bottom. The descent was simply miserable, especially knowing that we'd again failed the attempt to summit. I told the others that at least it was great to be in nature up on the mountain for a few days, but inside I hated that we hadn't made it to the top.

A year later, the four of us were heading back to Rainier. The night before we had all our gear laid out on Carl's living room floor. We discussed who would carry the common equipment, such as the tent, stove, and fuel. We made sure that we weren't missing anything important: ice axes, helmets, rope, crampons, harnesses, carabiners, prussic loops, food, water, headlamps, compasses, first aid, sleeping bags, and, of course, the needed layers of clothing.

All accounted for, we ate bananas, drank protein drinks and water, and began to discuss our level of commitment to the climb and the risks we would or would not take. As a group, we decided on the level of risk we were comfortable with. We prayed for good weather. At about midnight we said, "Cheers," with a last beer and clicked glasses to the optimistic success of the next day's climb.

When we got to the mountain early the next morning, the weather was good. Since there had been so much warm weather that summer, the crevasses were wide, and the climbing conditions on the mountain were much worse than normal with much more exposed rock.

We had a good start, seeing marmot, deer, and a black bear on the trek toward basecamp. We could also hear the rumble of the occasional avalanche and see the tumultuous icefalls high up on the mountain. We knew we'd have to be overly vigilant about the conditions. As we had expected, above Camp Muir as we crossed Ingram Flats, a few of the fixed aluminum ladders over large crevasses had been removed because they had become too unstable on the widening gaps. We had to circumvent the insanely long voids in the ice, adding a lot of distance to our climb.

When we reached the top of Disappointment Cleaver, we were all desperate for a rest. We hadn't slept in over twenty-four hours. Carl was stricken with some serious altitude sickness. He was vomiting. We decided to stop for a few hours, so we pulled out our sleeping bags and huddled together, shivering in the cold, along a flat ledge for about an hour and a half. As we lay there in the cold, it really wasn't as much about sleep as about being motionless and praying for the sun to come out and provide a bit of warmth and motivation.

Just as the sun was beginning to creep over the edges of the eastern sky with brilliant colors of orange and yellow, we packed up, tied the rope into our harnesses, and continued up. Back on the climb, it was precarious going. We had to traverse multiple fixed ladders across deep crevasses. At every ladder crossing, we had to have three of us spread out just right on the rope and be totally prepared to arrest if a fall occurred. The person crossing the wobbling aluminum ladder would have to look down, prepare steps in their mind, and walk as stably yet quickly as possible on the rungs of the ladder over the void below, which was often hundreds of feet down. In addition to the crevasses, we also had to climb much farther than normal across Ingram Glacier and onto Nisqually Glacier, crossing some very exposed sections with barely a nine-inch wide track along almost vertical faces.

Pushing up the mountain beyond exhaustion was certainly not easy, especially with the exceptionally difficult climbing conditions on Mt. Rainier that day. However, we knew that as long as the weather didn't hold us up, nothing would stop us from summing. At the start, during times of weakness, we'd draw encouragement from the commitment and cheers we had made as a group before the climb, but as time went on, motivation had to come from something even deeper.

During the climb, physical pain emanated from our now sore legs as we repeatedly stepped up steep slopes and climbed over giant rock formations with our heavy mountaineering boots and crampons. Heavy backpacks also provided a strain. It became difficult to get as much air as our bodies needed due to the lack of oxygen at that altitude. As we confronted these conditions, each of us began to examine our lives without those comforts that we typically enjoyed in our daily routines.

It was below freezing, but sweat soaked our hair. We had to sometimes take two breaths for every one step. Our minds raced to find comfort from distant places since there was no comfort during these moments on the mountain. For me, close friends and family were the main focus of my comfort. I longed to be back home in the coziness of my bed with my wife or playing on the living room floor with my kids. Feeling desperate from the agony of the climb, I was speaking to my wife in my head. I felt like we were actually communicating. I also dreamed of my young boys pushing themselves on a mountain expedition some day in the future. I was proud of them as I imagined their hard effort overcoming their own struggles. I felt a bit delirious, but I knew I loved my wife and my kids, and I couldn't wait to be with my family again. Enduring the climb made me appreciate these beautiful things, which are often taken for granted.

Upon reaching the 14,411-foot summit at Mt. Rainier's high point, Columbia Crest, we were all overcome with an elation from the joy of accomplishment. We smiled. We high-fived. We hugged. We brought out the football jersey of our deceased high school friend, Lewis, since we wanted him to be with us as well. We were overloaded with endorphins and other natural chemicals, which made all of us feel high. We enjoyed sharing the moment together. At the same time, we were also feeling an overwhelming affection for our loved ones back home—the ones who it felt like had helped us individually through the hardest parts of the struggle during the climb. It was a very powerful sensation, and we all felt connected and fully alive.

After a long rest in the summit crater, the descent proved incredibly difficult. We were all exhausted. The exposure along the nearly vertical sections was daunting, requiring extreme caution. We had to engender extra mental focus on certain sections where we were forced to put fixed anchors into the ice and belay each other across particularly dangerous obstacles. At some points, it would take us over an hour to move a mere fifty feet, but we made it.

In the end, it was an adventure of about nineteen miles, eighteen thousand feet of elevation gain and loss. It took us forty-two hours to complete our task. We did it on 1.5 hours of sleep. It was a horribly arduous and agonizing expedition for all of us—and it was wonderful ...

## *About You*

*Have you ever been exhausted to the point of almost being delirious? What were you doing and how did you feel during and afterwards?*

*How does being in pain or discomfort affect people's appreciation of the comforts they have in their lives?*

*Do Something Extraordinary*

*Intentionally put yourself in a challenging or exhausting situation, whether that be fasting for a day or running a marathon. During the discomfort, ask yourself what is really important to you.*

# FIFTEEN

# REFLECTIONS ON PURPOSE

Purpose is a tricky concept. First, it seems to have become almost synonymous with meaning, but really purpose is only one component of meaning (along with belonging, etc.). Second, when we think of purpose, we often think of a big, overarching plan or effort toward some lifetime achievement, like saving polar bears, providing clean water in remote villages, or having a planned direction in life. While purpose can be a grandiose cause, it can also be found in little bits of everyday life, like eating breakfast with a spouse, speaking with a colleague at work, or taking out the trash.

Another reason purpose is tricky is that, as shown by individuals including Immanuel Kant, William Damon, and Emily Esfahani Smith, purpose doesn't exist in a self-bubble, but rather involves contributing to the world and helping others. While striving toward an individual goal might engender positive emotions, it has been shown by Damon, for example, that only when something beyond the self is involved does purpose translate into a larger sense of meaning. Furthermore, meaning requires both internal and external factors. A key ingredient involved in recognizing purpose is understanding yourself. According to researcher Rebecca Schlegel, a primary step is people must know themselves in order to see the purpose in their path. Once the purpose is recognized, they become prepared to contribute to something beyond themselves and help others, which creates a larger sense of meaning.

Although identifying purpose takes introspection, looking inward isn't a solitary act as we need to consider our core assumptions as well as our relationships with others.

Self-reflection is a major part of self-discovery, but there are two additional factors necessary for "knowing thyself." The first is allowing ourselves time to think, which is the internal act of contemplating the self. The second is spending time with something, someone, some situation that is not us, not familiar, not comfortable, and meeting different types of people. This external component provides a contrastive spectrum of personalities, habits, and values, so we can consciously decide where we fit in, where we might want to be, and what our strengths and weaknesses might be. Ultimately, reflection about ourselves and our relationship with others can inspire us to determine where we might be able to make the most meaningful impact, thus resulting in an internal sense of purpose.

When I reflect on how purpose is evident in the narratives of my life, I realize that although I found purpose in my life, I'd been looking in the wrong direction. When I rode my bicycle from Washington State to California, for example, my goal was to get to Santa Barbara from Olympia on a pedal-bike. However, what this actually did was provide me miles and miles and hours and hours to examine myself. The result was recognizing purpose in my relationships and my value of the simplicity of life.

Similarly, my goal on Mt. Rainier was to reach the 14,411-foot summit, but climbing allowed me time for self-reflection and entailed my assisting the three climbers roped to me as it took a team effort to get to the summit. The idea of helping others became a reality on the mountain. We all realized that helping one another summit Rainier paralleled how we needed to help others in our daily routines as we attempted to reach higher places in life. In this way purpose would become more visible in our "regular" life experiences beyond the mountain.

My goal in moving to Thailand was to fight Muay Thai and to become a better boxer. Like riding my bike and climbing mountains, this was a goal for myself—an ego-driven goal. I became a better boxer, but reaching my boxing goal didn't provide purpose in my life; rather, I found purpose from meeting Thai people and spending time with them. It was loving and being loved by them that provided the meaning from that experience and pushed me toward a career of international programs. Witnessing the Thai people's affection and desire to help me equipped me to do the same for others, which, in the end, provided a recognizable purpose in my life leading to a larger sense of satisfaction and meaning.

It is interesting that reaching my self-centered goals did nothing to directly add purpose to my life. Instead the by-product of positioning myself in situations where people could help me was what added purpose as it allowed me to recognize how each kind act toward me was done intentionally and how positively these incidents affected me. From the old woman in Africa inviting me to sit and share a betel nut with her to the bikers sharing their massive fire-cooked feast to Naipon pulling me from the river, all of these tiny events were beautiful exchanges of one person helping a stranger with no agenda of receiving something in return. These small, beautiful moments encouraged me to act in a similar manner with others. From feeding my grandmother's cows to befriending Vladimir to pulling the Wayana infant from the river, these moments were natural extensions of what others had done for me. Brief moments helping others seems to possess an eternal goodness.

Purpose is a mindset that you can tap into to find meaning in the most simple and mundane things while connecting with something infinitely larger. An example in Esfahani Smith's book, *The Power of Meaning*, is a janitor at NASA in 1962. He didn't just go to work every day to clean toilets and take out the trash; rather, he went to work every day to help put a man on the moon. He performed his everyday duties with purpose, and in doing so, his actions provided a much greater reward that transcended himself.

### *About You*

*What are some everyday things that you do that have a larger purpose than you currently recognize? Have you taken the time to reflect on yourself, your goals, and things you are good at? Are there ways you could use these talents to contribute to something larger than yourself? What small step could you take to add a sense of purpose to your life? Extraordinary opportunities are waiting for you.*

*If you are inspired by something that you think might add an exciting new purpose in your life, I'd be happy to hear about it. You can reach me directly at* Erik@ErikSeversen.com.

# PART 3

# TRANSCENDENCE

*The abject humility we experience when we realize that we are nothing but tiny flecks in a vast and incomprehensible universe paradoxically fills us with a deep and powerful sense of meaning.*

—Emily Esfahani Smith

# SIXTEEN

# AURORA BOREALIS

*Alaska, USA. 1993. Twenty-Four Years Old*

As soon as I got the job offer, I knew Dave was the one to call. He is not only a great guy but is an adventurous spirit with a "why not?" mentality. At the time, Dave was living two states away in Los Angeles, and I was up near Seattle.

"Dave," I began when I called him on the phone, "I got a job in Alaska, and it starts in two weeks."

"Awesome, Erik," Dave replied, "Congratulations."

"I know, isn't that cool?" I continued, "But I'm not just calling to tell you about it. I need a ride."

"A ride to where?" Dave asked casually.

"To Alaska."

"To Al-a-a-s-s-ka?" Dave responded, drawing out the word as if to confirm that I really wanted him to drive over 3,500 miles to take me to work.

"Yes," I went on to say. "Wouldn't that be great?"

After the initial shock wore off, it didn't take more than a few moments for Dave to process the possibility. He cheerfully informed me, "Okay, I'll leave tomorrow morning."

Two and a half days later, Dave and I were packed up in his Suzuki Samurai soft-top mini-jeep heading north. We flew past the Space Needle and through the northern part of Washington State but were stalled at the border for a while. We declared that we had guns with us, so they wanted to check them out. While waiting, we passed a bit of time in the duty-free shop where we picked up a cheap fifth of Jack Daniels.

The jarring, potholed, teeth-shattering drive through Canada in the little jeep was also relatively quick. We knew we only had two weeks, and we wanted to accomplish two main things before I began work in Eagle River. One was to spend some time backpacking in the Alaska wilderness away from the jeep. The other was to make it all the way to Prudhoe Bay, which is a tiny outpost on the Arctic Ocean and the northernmost drivable point in North America.

As we were coming up on the Canada/Alaska border, we were reminiscing about all the deer, bears, moose, and other animals we had seen on the two-day trip through British Colombia and the Yukon. When we came upon a great big wooden sign that said, painted in fading Western script, "ALASKA, THE LAST FRONTIER," Dave and I were both taken aback. We decided to take a few photos of it. First, we made tough-man poses in front of the sign. Next, we got the guns out and made more poses. Then we got the bottle of whiskey out and took Wild West-inspired photos of each other holding up guns and chugging from the bottle. It was a hoot. We were still laughing when we drove up to the tiny wooden hut that served as the USA border inspection station.

Through a large sliding-glass window, the border agent asked for our ID.

"What are your plans while in Alaska?" the middle-aged, blonde-haired woman asked us in dry a voice.

"I got a job near Anchorage," I answered excitedly. "And my buddy is driving me up," I added even though I was behind the steering wheel at the time.

"How long did you stay in Canada?" the woman asked in a monotone.

"Oh, we just drove pretty much straight through," I told her, still excited to be entering "The Last Frontier."

"Did you buy anything while in Canada?" she continued.

Now, I'm not sure what popped into Dave's head to say this, but I think he was trying to add something to the conversation when he energetically answered, "Just a bottle of Jack Daniels that we bought at the duty-free store."

"Now, boys, you know you can't bring any duty-free items back into the USA. I'll need to take the bottle."

"Oh," I said trying to save our precious three-quarter-full bottle of Jack, "We finished it."

"You did, huh?" the woman said now starting to sound very austere. "You finished the bottle of Jack Daniels, did you? You just told me that you drove straight through."

"Uhh," I started to stammer also realizing that I reeked of booze from when we'd been taking the photos. I looked at Dave for support or for an idea.

"Well?" the woman pressed, "You're either smuggling liquor, or you're drunk drivers. Which do you want it to be?"

"Uhh," I said again. "Um," I continued. "We just took pictures in front of the sign," I uttered in desperation, not answering the question.

I was going to keep talking, but the woman at the border hut looked hard at us for a moment, handed back our IDs, and just waved us through. She actually had a final bit of pep in her voice and a slight smile when she said, "Enjoy Alaska, boys." I guess she didn't feel up to the hassle of figuring out exactly what was going on and decided that we were in a remote enough area that we wouldn't be able to cause too much trouble. That and I think she actually thought that the predicament she caught us in was a bit funny as well.

Having successfully been vetted and approved worthy of Alaska, we continued on and later stopped in a tiny junction town called Tok. We ended up stashing the jeep in some remote area off the road and did a three-day trek through the bush to stretch our legs, clear our heads, and explore. At one point, we were in a bit of an uncomfortably thick section of birch trees and thickets. Dave was carrying a 20-gauge, .22 Mag over-under rifle that my grandfather left me in his will. I had a .44 Magnum revolver in a holster around my waist.

As we fought our way through the brush, an ungodly explosion of sound suddenly sent shock waves through both of us. The sound was from something crashing through the bushes. Two images simultaneously appeared in my head. One was the image of a large deer rushing away from us through the bush, and the other was that of a large bear rushing toward us. I unconsciously pulled out the .44, not thinking that in this brush I'd never get a shot off if we were being charged. I looked at Dave who was also petrified, stone white, and holding the rifle in no particular direction.

"Did you hear that?" I asked him.

It was now silent. We both laughed at my ridiculous question since it just sounded like a building had crashed to the ground around us—something there's no way anyone could miss.

"Yep," Dave confirmed with a nervous smile.

"Oh my gosh," I continued, still holding the gun out stupidly and shaking to my bones, "What in the world *was* that?"

As we continued up a few feet further to the summit of a small clearing, we saw a giant bull moose thrashing through the brush. He was charging up a hill away from us.

After the shock, Dave and I were both nervous for hours. Finally, we found a large, mosquito-free clearing with a soft bed of peat where we set up camp. Fatigued by the long hike through swampy bogs, thick brush, and the exertion of adrenalin from our scare, we went to bed early and slept like we were tucked into a perfectly comforting child's cradle the size of the planet.

The next day we were proud of ourselves that with only a compass and a map, we emerged from the woods within a hundred yards of the jeep we had left days earlier on our circular mini-expedition. We then continued north and stopped in Fairbanks for a few more supplies, including the extra gas cans we'd need to make it along the remote Dalton Highway, which was nothing more than four hundred miles of gravel connecting the world to a very northern dot on the map.

Wide and expansive was pretty much our view for the next few days. The beautiful monotony was broken up by the many caribou we saw on the tundra, the occasional muskox, and a tiny sign that stated that we were entering the Arctic Circle. Other than that, there was nothing. The feeling was spectacular.

After reaching our goal of hitting Prudhoe Bay, we turned around and headed back south. While I didn't feel like I was pushing the jeep harder than normal, I was driving relatively fast. I enjoyed the boat-like feel of the soft road as the jeep swayed back and forth in the gravel. This was nice … until I lost control. The jeep swerved back and forth until one of its tires popped on a jagged rock. Once the corner of the jeep dropped, I knew instantly that the tire was punctured. I stopped in the middle of the empty road.

"Dave," I intoned, "Wake up. We've got a flat."

After waking Dave, I flipped the little latch on the canvas door. That's when I felt the furious tailwind I'd been driving in. As soon as the latch on my door unlocked, the wind caught the door, ripped it off the jeep, and blew it about fifty yards in front of us until it got stuck in a rut. The wind felt like it was blowing a hundred miles per hour. Somehow, with a lot of teamwork, we got the tire changed and continued.

Once we were below the Arctic Circle, both the temperature and the landscapes were nearer to standards that humans can enjoy. We found another good spot to pull off the road and explore. We stashed the jeep, stuffed our backpacks, and went out into the wild. We loved these times.

As we walked, it was as if every word spoken was a secret, and there was no need for discussions about "how your day was" or "what the weather was." We were sharing the same experience and we knew how the other person's day was going and we knew exactly what the weather was, so do you want to know what happened? Profound conversations. Conversations that are often hidden below layers and layers and layers of being busy in our elaborate normal lives. The depth of the things we spoke about seemed normal in the tranquility of nature, and we enjoyed stripping our souls naked in front of each other, revealing both epic dreams of the future as well as ruminations about the past, about prideful discretions as well as our insecurities that somehow matched the uncertainty of our long treks across wild regions, which, no matter how much preparation we had, held our lives in its hands.

After a long morning of hiking, Dave and I found an area that felt particularly wonderful. It was a combination of trees and open areas. There was a slight breeze that kept bothersome mosquitoes away. Dave and I intentionally brought rice and bread with us, but we didn't bring any meat. With an idealistic vision, we wanted to survive as much as possible off the land we were visiting. This kept us engaged with our surroundings in the quest for sustenance.

"Let's try over here," Dave suggested, as I was looking at the compass. We were deciding between two valleys.

Dave definitely made the right decision. After picking up large caribou antlers and holding them to our heads pretending we were animals, we were still laughing when we came upon a shallow river with hundreds and hundreds of salmon swimming upstream. I think they were all there: king, coho, sockeye, pink. We stood in awe for a few moments before getting out the fishing gear. It only took one large chinook to provide a bountiful feast of luscious salmon cooked over a fire and seasoned with lemon, salt, and pepper.

Salmon wasn't the only protein we found. We also hunted ptarmigan with the shotgun. It was amazing to enter that point of connection to the serenity of the mountains and hills as we attempted to stealthily find our dinner while at the same time mindfully attempting not to surprise a grizzly. Even though we had a shotgun and a .44 Magnum revolver that Dave and I alternated carrying, we certainly did not feel at the top of the food chain while in the bush.

It was after a particularly lovely meal that Dave and I finally cracked open the Jack Daniels for the first time since the border sign. We were drinking just enough to become a bit giddy. We were sitting outside of our tent as the late evening was turning into dark night.

That's when I looked up to see a long whitish-blue band across the sky. First, I thought that I might have had too much to drink, so I closed my eyes for a moment to clear them. Then I looked up again. The strange band was still there. I was just about to tell Dave about it when my mind exploded with the surprise of the technicolored display in front of me.

"Oh my gosh," I said, almost in a whisper to Dave, whose back was to the northern sky. "Look," I calmly continued, as if not to disturb the spectacle. "Look," I repeated almost as if to confirm to myself that what I was seeing was real.

"Wow," Dave uttered in a soft voice that betrayed his normally loud tenor.

"Is that the Northern Lights?" I asked as if under a spell.

"The Aurora Borealis," Dave mumbled, mesmerized.

And that was all we said.

The spectacle was like God had taken hold of the band across the sky with both hands and shook it, waving up and down a technicolored electric sheet. The colors were of not only blue, but every shade of blue, with turquoise being very prominent; and not only red, but every shade of red, with scarlet being the most prominent. Other shards of yellow, green, and orange also flashed across the sky as the images bounced up and down, dancing in the heavens.

I have no idea how long we stared or how long the spectacle lasted. We both felt hypnotized by it until a small mouse darted across the small clearing near our fire. The little mouse was more interested in exploring the foreign smells and items Dave and I had brought into its northern home than with the inspiring show in the sky.

*What does the mouse think of the show?* I wondered.

I felt very small myself as if I had somehow witnessed the edge of the universe for the first time.

## *About You*

*Have you ever been inspired by nature to the point of awe? Where was it and what was the feeling like?*

*What are some natural places that come to mind that have an awe-inspiring effect on people?*

*Do Something Extraordinary*

*Intentionally decide to find something amazing in nature—whether it be going to a dark spot out of the city to stare at the stars, visiting the ocean, or examining a big tree in your own yard. While gazing, just soak in the feeling of one-ness we share with nature.*

# SEVENTEEN

## MACHINE GUN IN LAGOS

*Nigeria, Africa. 1989. Twenty Years Old*

The first thing I noticed was the end of the machine gun's metallic taste. The policeman holding its barrel in my mouth was shouting at me. I was paralyzed with the fear of being killed, but was also strangely nervous that my front teeth might chip on the tarnished black metal barrel if he pulled the trigger.

"You are a spy!" he screamed close to my face looking down into my eyes. Sweat covered the skin on his ebony face, which was wide and wrinkled with intensity. His eyes were red. His red gums showed above his white teeth as he snarled.

"No" was all I could manage to utter, as the sight at the end of the gun touched the roof of my mouth. I then tasted gunpowder as well.

"Why didn't you stop at the checkpoint then?" he spat in barely comprehensible pidgin English.

I wanted to answer, but like trying to speak to a dentist when asked a question while he's working inside your mouth, I didn't know exactly what to do. I tried to mumble that I wasn't a spy.

I was sitting cross-legged as instructed in the small hut at the side of the road wondering what I was supposed to do. I looked up at him. I wasn't calm, and I couldn't move.

"I should shoot you right now!" he continued, spitting on my face as he yelled.

His green uniform should have been a sign of comfort for me, but this policeman was certainly not my protector. I began to tremble as his threats to kill me continued.

"Killing is easy," he explained, "No one cares about you here."

Uncontrollably, my body began to shake. I nervously scanned the dirt floor of the hut for signs of blood to see if anyone else in this position might not have made it out on two feet. A minute went by until he backed up a few inches still pointing the gun at my face.

"What are you doing here?" he demanded—yet again.

"*Je suis un touriste,*" I responded in bad French.

"I speak English! Why don't you speak English to me?" he inquired viciously.

I had been traveling for months in North Africa speaking French, so the sudden entry into English-speaking Nigeria hadn't clicked in my brain. On top of this, in shock, I could barely understand his English anyway.

"I'm sorry. I'm sorry," I replied. "I'm nervous, and I've only been speaking French for a long time."

He kept insisting I was a spy, never taking the gun off me. Only after over about an hour of questioning, did his intense anger begin to calm a bit.

I had become weary of African border crossings. Already along the Morocco-Algeria frontier I'd been interrogated, but nothing like this. At that crossing the discussion was over whether Algeria should let me in since my long hair didn't match the photo in my passport, but that was mostly it.

I ended up hitching a ride in Algeria with a group of French. They were driving three old cars down from France and through the Sahara to sell them in Togo. We were two days into the seven-day trip through the vast Sahara when they started telling me of the notorious Algeria-Niger border crossing. It was in the middle of the desert at a place called In Guezzam.

"Since there is virtually nothing but sand for a thousand miles in any direction, anyone who crosses is at the mercy of the border guards," one of the French told me. "Most people don't have enough supplies to turn around and head back north through the desert, so they are stuck," the French guy continued. "It is really about bribes. They select a different policeman each week to man the deserted crossing, and in that dusty week, the officer receives more money in 'gifts' than he makes throughout the rest of the year with his salary."

The French guy then asked me, "You've got everything in order, right?"

Immediately, I felt sick. I had forgotten about the declaration form that I had had to complete while entering Algeria. I had innocently exchanged some American dollars for Algerian franks with a person whom I had met and stayed with near Algiers. My documents were now *not* in order because the amounts of US dollars listed on my customs declarations forms did not match the amount of US dollars I had listed on my bank exchange papers. This was a serious violation, and I didn't have enough money for a viable bribe to get through. For two days, I could think of nothing but the up-coming border crossing. I spent a lot of time silently praying about this.

As we approached the small house and gate that stood in the middle of the sandy expanse, I was shaking with the idea that I'd be stuck in this place. I prayed harder. All of us were asked to get out of the cars, and the police began asking us questions. That's when it all went down.

"You—come with me," the head guard ordered me.

I followed him into a room with blue paint peeling off the white walls. Flies were buzzing everywhere. I sat on a metal folding chair across from the small metal desk.

The uniformed guard with an un-buttoned collar stated, "Papers."

I handed him my blue passport and declaration form.

He leaned back in his chair.

When he looked at the American passport, he leaned forward to comment, "America. I like America. George Bush!" He then smiled and laughed. He laughed some more and repeated that he liked George Bush.

"Okay," he said.

"Yeah," I responded.

*Is that it?* I thought to myself. I wondered if I was somehow being set up. Even still, I stood up and reached across the desk, shaking the guard's hand.

He handed back to me my passport and documents without even opening the passport. I thanked him. He reminded me to check in with the police every day I was in Niger as was required by the visa, which he also hadn't even looked at.

I thanked him and quickly walked out of the shade of the office and into the scorching sun. I waited for the French to finish the inspection of their cars and papers.

All the Frenchmen had been nervous for me since I had told them about my papers not being in order, so that evening we celebrated at the camp we set up by splurging with spaghetti cooked in a large aluminum pot over an open fire in front of our tents. Excited to have the first real meal in days, when the Parmesan cheese was passed around, I sprinkled a generous amount of it over my noodles. Karma got back at me for the greedy move; when I took my first bite, I realized that it was not Parmesan, but a large tub of salt. I never told any of the French and ate the horrid-tasting plate to gain from the much-needed nutrition, but it certainly wasn't the great meal I had been looking forward to.

I continued with the French all the way to Benin before heading east into Nigeria. Crossing the border from Benin to Nigeria was a nightmare itself with hundreds of people and seemingly as many guards squeezing through different gates, lines, and wooden tables. There was mud everywhere.

The whole scene was a din of people yelling orders and others arguing and fighting. When I finally found where I was supposed to go, I handed my completed declaration form to a guard in a makeshift plywood kiosk. The guard asked to see my money, so I handed him everything I had, which was $200 US dollars and a few Central African Francs from Benin. The guard decided to count the money below the desk.

"No, this is wrong," the guard informed me. "You wrote that you have $200 USD, but there are only $150 here.

"No way," I replied. I knew exactly how much money I had because I was calculating every cent and carefully spending less than $50 per month on the trip through Africa. "That can't be," I repeated.

When he handed the money back, of course, I counted $150. He scribbled over the $200 I had entered on the form and quickly changed it to the $150 he insisted was there. Obviously, he'd pocketed the rest.

Once through the prison-like border crossing and into Nigeria I walked very far to where my shared taxi, with the five other African riders in it, was waiting for me. I apologized for taking so long because random guards kept checking my pack and asking for bribes, which I'd mostly held out on.

It must have been over an hour that the others were waiting for me, so the mood of the taxi was mostly frustration with a bit of impatient anger in the mix. With six riders and a driver, the small car was already packed, smelly, and steaming hot as we rolled along dirt roads lined with rich green jungles.

I had thought that crossing the border would be it, but every few hundred yards, there was another checkpoint. Each became the same. In either a blue, green, or camo uniform with a collar, the guards would eye us as we approached, walk toward the car when it slowed, and then hold a hand up signaling for us to stop. They'd then walk right up to the car, peer in at me, the only white person in the car, and order, "Get out." They'd then question me and make me get my pack out from the trunk. If I gave a small bribe, we'd be fine, but when I was running out of all money except for my hidden $150, it would take a long time to finally be allowed to proceed. This went on for what seemed like hours, and everyone in the taxi was furious. I also felt bad but couldn't do a thing.

Sick and tired of this game, as we began to approach another checkpoint, the driver yelled something. All the people in the car started arguing in a Bantu language. It was a chaotic and heated discussion. As we neared the checkpoint, I began to understand what it was about. The driver didn't begin to slow as we approached. He even began to speed up. As we were right next to the guard at the side of the road, our driver hit the gas pedal and moved to the far left of the wet dirt road. The guard at the side of the road ran behind us shouting something at the top of his lungs, and *pop, pop, pop* came the sound of him shooting his rifle in the air.

Simultaneously another guard ran out ahead of us and threw a spiked board across the road just in front of us. It was nothing more than an eight-foot two-by-four with nails sticking out of it, but it was certainly enough for the driver to have to slam on the brakes. We slid on the slick road, stopping inches before the board. The three guards came running over to us with assault rifles aimed at us. They commenced screaming at us, ordering that we all get out of the car. After about thirty seconds of loud yelling back and forth between the guards, taxi driver, and others, the head guard thrust his gun at me. He commanded in pidgin English that I go into a small hut and kneel on the floor.

As he put the gun in my face roaring that I was a spy, one of the other guards came in with my tan army-style backpack that I'd gotten at a military surplus store back in the United States. During the interrogation, they dumped out the contents of my pack and sifted through everything a few times. Once the main guard who hadn't left me in over an hour started to calm, he began going through my pack with more care and order. Luckily, I had hidden my American dollars in a small pocket that I had sewn into my boxer shorts.

Finally, the guard, who was now also sitting across from me in the dark hut, laid his gun on the floor and announced, "No, I don't think you are a spy. No, I like Americans. Americans like to give me gifts." As he said this, he placed my small green tent and my large hunting knife between us in an obvious gesture to communicate that I had the choice to keep one item and the other would go to him. I immediately reached out and picked up my hunting knife. The guard picked up the tent, gathered his rifle, and walked out. It was obvious that the episode was over, so I quickly packed up my gear, threw one side of the shoulder straps of the heavy pack over my right shoulder, and walked back to the car where the shared taxi driver and passengers were waiting. Without speaking, we put my pack in the trunk, squished into the car, and began to drive away.

"Wait, wait, wait, wait!" the head guard called, jogging toward us. We stopped. He looked through the open side window of the car and told me, "You have to come back and show me how to set it up."

I couldn't believe it. I looked back toward the hut and saw the nylon tent on the ground and a few poles lying next to it. The car just stayed there in the middle of the road, idling, as I was forced to go set up the tent before returning.

I felt exhausted by fright and spent adrenalin as the car finally crept away from this checkpoint, heading toward Lagos.

As we entered Lagos, I began to have a very uneasy feeling as I took in the enormous crowds of people, the exposed sewers running along the side of the road, and the extreme poverty. The car became like a beacon of gravity attracting groups of people who followed alongside the car. They were yelling things, trying to sell things, or just curiously following us with their hands on the car as we slowed. One of the passengers in the car told me not to have my arm on the edge of the open window because someone would try to snatch the watch off my wrist. The scene became worse and worse as we finally entered the large dirt parking lot of the taxi and bus station, which was nothing more than a clearing of dirt and mud full of cars, trucks, and dirty minivans.

We piled out of the car, and the spent passengers began to walk away. I stood at the trunk of the car when my driver walked around to the back holding onto the keys and intentionally not opening the trunk. He flatly told me, "Give me 50,000 CFA." Totally exhausted and emotionally beaten,

I handed him 30,000 CFA, all I had left. He opened the trunk, and I grabbed my pack.

Evidently one of the passengers from the taxi saw this. He was a large black man with a dirty and wrinkled silver suit and brown shoes. He walked back over to me and asked, "What are you going to do now?"

I answered, "Go to the bank, exchange some money, and get out of Lagos as quickly as I can."

He simply shook his head back and forth and said, "Today is Sunday. The banks are closed. I haven't seen my family in five years, but if I don't take you home with me, you'll be dead before morning."

I really didn't know what to say other than thank you, which I did.

I followed him. As we began walking down a small dirt alley surrounded by shanti houses, he had another idea. Rather than ruining his reunion with his family, we walked up to the house of one of his friends, Abaeze, whom he also hadn't seen in five years. He explained the situation to the friend's family. The family warmly welcomed me—the white, dirty, broken stranger—into their home. I ended up staying with this wonderful family for three days.

Abaeze taught me about the city and even helped me exchange money at the bank, where they insisted that I exit through the back door, so I wouldn't be mugged in front of the bank.

When it came time to travel on, at 6 am Abaeze left me in a small minivan headed toward Cameroon. He arranged for the driver to have me share the front seat with one other passenger. As we finally began to pull out of the dirty parking lot in the early morning coolness, an agitated man in a uniform and M16 rifle started screaming in front of our van. He looked right at me, pointed his gun at me for a quick moment, then held it in the air and fired one shockingly loud round that echoed and made my ears ring. To this day, I have no idea what that was about, but it was certainly a reminder of the Lagos I had entered three days earlier.

Happily, the time I spent with Abaeze, his wife, Abidemi, and their three lovely children made the entire saga of coming to Nigeria an amazing and positive experience. Though I am still haunted by the checkpoint episode from time to time, my thoughts of Lagos remain of great meals, fun, and storytelling in the gracious home of a wonderful Nigerian family.

### About You

*Have you ever been faced with a violent situation that was out of your control? If so, what happened?*

*Is it true that something good can come from every situation, or are there things that can happen that have absolutely no positive take-away?*

*Do Something Extraordinary*

*Think of someone who is going through a difficult situation and look for a positive outcome from the bad situation. While being sensitive to their situation, see if there is a way to share or highlight the positive aspect with them. Try to do this yourself, should you find yourself in difficulty.*

# EIGHTEEN

# CHOLERA

*Morocco, Africa. 1989. Twenty Years Old*

I was leaving a remote Berber village where I had spent four magical days. However, I made a big mistake as I was leaving: I was offered un-boiled water from a well, and I accepted it. I knew to watch out for untreated well water, so I mostly drank from the plastic bottles of water that I carried with me, or I drank boiled water. On the day I was leaving, however, an elderly man desperately wanted me to sit with him for a moment. He anxiously wanted to give me the gift of some water. Not wanting to offend him, I drank a bit of it. Later, I would desperately pay for it. This kind old man's gift nearly killed me.

I made it through the whole day, trudging along under the sun with my heavy backpack. Near the end of the day of walking, I could sense that something was wrong. My stomach began not to feel right. I stopped a bit earlier than normal and decided to set up my camp. Within the half hour when I was sitting and resting before digging my tent out of my pack, I became violently ill. I vomited before I even unpacked my tent.

Setting up the tent was extremely difficult. Every time I exerted myself even a little bit, I'd feel sick. I finally got the tent up, but as soon as I crawled inside, I had to get out again. The extreme cramping in my stomach told me that I was now beyond just vomiting. Diarrhea was next.

Miles and miles from the nearest person, I didn't feel ashamed in stripping off my pants and crawling out naked. I didn't make it far from the tent when my whole body constricted. I shot liquid from every opening in my body. The diarrhea and projectile vomit mirrored each other out of each end of my body as I agonized on my hands and knees in the sand. I must have repeated this revolting act ten or twenty times.

My head felt like it would explode. My stomach cramped with intense pain. Tears shot from my eyes and snot from my nose as I gagged and prayed for it to stop. Finally came a tiny bit of relief. I cleaned myself with the precious water I had with me.

I'd left the Berber village with five two-liter bottles. That was plenty of water to walk the forty miles between the Berber village and Alnif, but I hadn't expected to use so much to clean up. Plus, being so sick, I certainly wasn't thinking straight.

I spent the entire night in and out of my tent. When the sun started to peek over the edge of the sandy horizon, I found myself lying exhausted in a patch of sand absolutely surrounded by vomit and watery shit. I just lay there in agony, wanting the sun to come out.

As soon as the sun was up, I already wished for the cool of the night. The warmth made me feel worse. I used more water to clean up when I realized that I only had one bottle of water remaining. Fear should have struck me, but I just found it mildly disturbing.

I desperately wanted to stay in that spot and not move, but I knew that I'd die without water. I knew that I was already horribly dehydrated. I forced myself into action and sloppily stuffed my tent, unfolded, into my large backpack. I never left trash in the wild while traveling through Africa, but on this occasion, I didn't even consider picking up the empty plastic water bottles that littered the sand.

As soon as I began walking, I was overcome by the weight of my backpack. I had to rest after only a few yards and then started again. After stopping a second and third time, I was delirious. I started hallucinating and mumbling out loud to myself about my predicament. I was both terrified and apathetic at the same time. In my desperation to lighten my pack, I threw out an umbrella I was carrying; then I threw out a loaf of bread; then I took out my few cans of food and threw them into the sand, totally unaware that these actions would leave me even more helpless.

I trudged on for I don't know how long. My water was down to about a cupful. At least I wasn't still vomiting, but my stomach and head ached. I just pressed on. I was saddened by the fact that I had left the comfort of the Berber village, and I missed the people desperately. I knew that I'd never see them again. I was wondering if I would never see any of my family and friends again as well, but I missed the Berbers most because they were most recent in my hampered memory.

Looking up at the sun, I felt like I was being called to stop and rest, but I pulled my white turban tighter around my face and kept going. Then, my mind started playing tricks on me. I started hearing a strange noise. The noise became louder and louder. I wondered what it was when I finally turned to see a man on a moped-like motorcycle. I was immediately terrified that he would ride past me. I laboriously put my hand up to stop him. He pulled up next to me. As a second beaten-up motorcycle arrived, I uttered in desperation, *"Je suis très malade,"* meaning, "I'm very sick."

The man on the motorcycle could tell that I wasn't in good shape. He got off, took my pack, and tied it to the back of the other small motorcycle. He motioned for me to get onto the back of his bike. I think I might have told them that I was going to Alnif, but it didn't really matter because there was nowhere else to go along the small path we were on. It was slow going, riding through the sand, but the movement and the breeze and the fact that I knew I was safe made me feel much better.

When we entered Alnif, the guys took me to the only hotel in town, which was a cinderblock, four-room building with peeling blue and white walls. They helped me arrange a room and told me to rest. They also told me that they only traveled along that path to Alnif once a week, and that other than the two of them, the path was utterly unused. Still terribly weak, I simply thanked them profusely.

The owner of the hotel was very kind. He walked me over to the first open room and sent a young man to get me some medicine. When the young man returned, however, he didn't want to leave me alone. He was intrigued by the foreigner from the USA who was now staying in his small town. He kept talking and talking. I tried to give as many hints as I could that I wanted to be alone to rest, but no hints were taken. Then, as I was unpacking a few things from my bag, he saw the chemical mace that I carried with me.

"Great," he said in French, "Bug spray." He pointed the small canister up toward the line of insects crawling on the ceiling and unleashed the powerful mace into the room. He looked shocked, covered his eyes, and then coughed as he rushed out of the room.

I was delighted that he was gone though there was now mace in the room. I pulled the covers over my head and buried myself into the darkness of the blankets, begging for relief. It came in the form of sleep. I slept and slept for almost two days until I finally felt good again.

As I checked out of the hotel, I noticed the small town for the first time. I enjoyed its dusty charm. I had no desire to walk any longer, so I arranged a ride east toward the Algerian frontier.

As I left Alnif, we passed the sandy path I had come from. I thought of the two guys on the motorcycles. I thanked God for the miraculous fact that they had been travelling on a Wednesday.

## About You

*Have you ever been sick to the point of becoming delirious? If so, when was it and did you have any strange thoughts or visions during it?*

*How has modern medicine changed the way we live our lives?*

Do Something Extraordinary

*Think of someone you know who has survived a life-threatening illness. Ask if they'd be willing to share with you any transformational moments when they somehow viewed the world differently during or after their condition. Ask them if they intentionally changed anything in their lives because of the experience.*

# NINTEEN

# RAINBOW GATHERING

*Oregon, USA. 1989. Nineteen Years Old*

McDonald's was a kind of funny place to meet, but it was near the freeway, off I-5 just south of Tacoma. I arrived early and plopped down on a well-cut lawn. I dug a book out of my faded-green army duffle bag.

The free "on the road" feeling started to sink in as I opened the book right to an old lottery ticket I was using as a bookmark. The sun was warm on my face, and I sensed the joy of the children as they walked past me with their sheepish grins and uninhibited stares. My unkempt mid-length hair, homemade tie-dyed shirt, love beads, and worn jeans did make me stand out a bit.

A woman about forty years old and beautiful sat on the lawn near me. She sat close to show me, and perhaps to show McDonald's patrons, that my attire did not offend her. Her naturalness suggested that she too at one time had been a teenage hippie who sat around parking lots and grassy areas waiting for rides.

"Hey, hey you, hey, HEY!" I heard from behind me. I knew it was my ride calling me on the second "hey." I also realized that Melody probably had forgotten my name. We had met at a party a few weeks earlier, and she and a friend agreed to give me a ride down to Eugene for a Rainbow Gathering. I could have turned around, but I wanted her to come to me. I wanted her to come up beside me, so I could casually look up from my book and greet her. The book was a thick novel by Ayn Rand that might impress her.

"Hey, how are you?" she greeted me, a bit out of breath. I looked up and unconsciously took off my clear-framed cat eye reading glasses. She was stunning. I immediately forgot all about my book. Melody was wearing a loose white summer dress, and her hair was braided in cornrows with hundreds of tiny copper bells hanging on the end of each braid.

"Hi," I said as I rose and placed my arms around her. "Where's the car?"

"Oh, it's on the freeway. We thought it would be easier for me to just walk up instead of taking the exit."

We met Chrystal at the car. She and I greeted each other with a long tight hug, which symbolized the unity and love that we felt in life and in the air of the day. I broke off the embrace with a quick peck on her cheek and entered the back seat of the small, rusting car. We pulled out into the flow of traffic and spoke of our excitement for the Oregon County Fair and Rainbow Gathering. The noise of the warm wind soon drowned our shallow conversation, so I laid back onto my pack and an old blue and white ice chest. The breeze felt soft on my face, and I soon was dozing. Even still, I managed to hear the faint sound of Jethro Tull playing out of the front speaker of the car.

Wakened by the change in speed and momentum, I slowly lifted myself to a sitting position and saw that we were off the freeway.

"Where are we?" I asked.

"I don't know, about halfway between Olympia and Portland, I guess. Were you asleep the whole time? We were so loud."

"Yea, it felt great," I said. "I didn't get much sleep last night. Where are we going?"

"Get gas and Melody has to go pee," Chrystal replied.

The car rolled to a stop at a Chevron station. We piled out laughing at how Chrystal had parked, about six feet away from the pump and at an awkward angle. I slipped on my sandals and headed across the greasy parking lot toward a faded door, which said, "ME," on it since the "N" was missing.

When I came out of the small, dingy bathroom, I noticed a few changes in the scenery. First, the hood of Chrystal's car was up, bad sign. Second, there was a blue Nova in the parking lot with two longhairs sitting on the hood. I decided I should go over to Chrystal's car first.

"What's wrong with the car?" I asked with an uneasy smile.

"Oh, nothing. It just needs a little oil," Chrystal responded.

*A little oil*, I thought as I saw two empty cartons and two full ones sitting on the dirty engine, waiting their turns. I could have helped, but Chrystal looked so beautiful leaning over the motor, one hand on the top of the fender, the other flawlessly pouring the third quart of oil into the small black opening.

Melody came walking out of the station with an armload of food and tossed it through the open car window.

"You guys going to the fair?" I asked the guys on the Nova.

"Yea, what about you?"

"If the mechanic gets the car going," I replied, glancing at Chrystal who amusingly peeked around the open hood and playfully stuck her tongue out at me.

"Where are you guys from?" I asked, looking at the guy in a blue and black tie-dye.

"Bellingham."

"Where are you staying tonight?" I continued.

"Who knows, man. I hope we can stay on the grounds."

"Good luck," I said. Chrystal slammed the hood, and we got into the car. "See you there, maybe," I said, as we drove out of the lot.

It was fun to begin to see more and more people obviously heading toward the weeklong gathering of hippies and travelers. The Oregon County Fair, Rainbow Gathering, and Grateful Dead concert were being talked about as the biggest events of the year.

A few hours later, we entered Eugene. It was getting dark, and we still needed to find a camping spot for the night.

Unexpectedly, I smelled something and asked, "Does anyone smell anything?"

"No," they replied.

Then I heard a faint noise. "Does anyone hear anything? I asked.

"No."

Then I felt something. "Ouch!" I screamed as I jumped sideways, almost into the driver's seat. I found myself slapping the back of my shoulder with my left hand, burning it along with my back, but at least I'd extinguished the rapidly growing small flame. "I thought I got stung by a bee," I explained.

"What happened?" Chrystal asked, laughing.

"I don't know. Something burned me," I replied, as I showed them the hole in my shirt.

Melody started laughing hysterically and informed us, "I thought it fell out the window."

"What fell out?" I responded.

It took Melody a minute to control her laughing. Then she answered, "My cigarette. I dropped it about a minute ago. I thought it went out the window."

"You did it on purpose," I said, making a bigger deal of it than it was. Next I pulled the lever on the side of my seat and slammed the seat down, smashing Melody's legs and squishing her in the tiny back seat. I took advantage of her restricted movement by tickling her until her face turned bright red and she couldn't breathe.

"That will teach you to light me on fire," I commented, laughing as we sped along the road looking for campgrounds.

"All filled," a thin man at the horse camp entrance said. "Try Circle Lake campground. It is kind of far out, but it might not be full."

"Thanks," I said. We backed our way out along the thin wooded road. We passed a VW bus packed with people whom we recognized as fellow fair-goers.

We tried every campground within ten miles of Eugene with no luck getting a place to bed down.

"Do you know how to get to the fairgrounds, Chrystal?" I asked.

"No, what about you, Melody?"

Melody slowly shook her head but kept her eyes on the road as if looking for help on where to go.

"What's that?" Melody asked.

"A hitchhiker," I answered. "He's obviously going to the fair."

"Pick him up, Chrystal," Melody recommended.

"Do we have room?"

"Of course. Melody can sit back on my lap," I responded. Chrystal pulled off the road, and Melody opened the door.

"You going to the fair?" Melody asked the bearded black man with love beads, a leather jacket, and a colorful backpack.

"Yeah."

"Do you know where it is?" Chrystal asked.

"Yeah. I worked there last year. It's not too far," he responded.

"Good." Melody handed his backpack to me and then followed it into the cramped back seat. The Jimi Hendrix look-a-like got in the front.

"My name is Clark," I said as I awkwardly tried to reach my hand around the right side of Melody and left side of the front passenger seat. Clark isn't my real name, but it's the name I was called at Grateful Dead shows and the name most people at the gathering would know me by.

"Mine is Jim," he said, and he softly grabbed my hand.

"Jew," I stated.

"Jim," he corrected.

"Oh, it is good to meet you, Joe," I erroneously responded, truly not hearing his name correctly.

"Yeah, okay," Jim said with a chuckle.

We drove ahead into the darkness. As time passed, it grew silent, and Melody grew heavy on my lap. After digging his hand into his jacket pocket, Jim pulled out a plastic sandwich bag half-full of marijuana. He opened it and placed a bit in a small wooden pipe and lit it. As he placed it to his lips, there was a long sound of rushing air, then total, complete silence for a few seconds, followed by another sound as he released the trapped smoke from his lungs. The car filled with the unique scent.

"You want some?" he asked as he looked at Chrystal.

"No thanks, I'm okay," she replied.

"What about you, Clark?"

*Just a little*, I thought, *to be friendly*.

"Sure," I said quickly as I reached out for the pipe. I held the pipe with my left hand, which was around Melody, and lit the end of the pipe with my right hand, which was also around Melody. My face pressed against Melody's cheek in the cramped back seat. She smiled widely as I inhaled the fumes a few inches from her face.

"You want some?" I asked Melody.

"No thanks," she said.

I handed the pipe back to Jim who opened the window and flicked the ashes out onto the road.

"Where are you from?" I asked Jim.

"All over."

"How long have you been on the road?"

"Bout seven years, I guess," he answered.

"Do you come to the fair every year?"

"For about twenty years," he said with a smile on his face. "A lot of nice people," he continued, "and this year is going to be a spectacular gathering. I even know people from New York who are coming."

The ride once again grew silent. I couldn't stop wondering what Chrystal and Melody were thinking as my mind began to drift. I wanted to reach up and pat Jim on the shoulder as a small token of appreciation for the little pick-me-up he had given me, but I couldn't reach. I briefly rubbed Melody's knee with the end of my fingers instead. Still inches away, she turned her head toward me and smiled, knowing that I was enjoying my thoughts.

We finally pulled into a large field, which was the parking area for the fair. It was mostly dark now. Jim thanked us for the ride and left to register for work. The two girls and I followed people around, wondering where we should go and where we were going to sleep that night.

The parking lot was magical itself. Cars, buses, and trucks from everywhere in the country were there. Many people were present, doing a variety of things from making love to selling handmade crafts.

"Do you have a pass?" asked a man with long brown hair.

"No, we just got in. We don't know where we are going to stay yet," I explained.

"A lot of people are trying to sneak into the grounds tonight, but it is kind of difficult," he told me.

"Why aren't they letting everyone in like they always have?" Chrystal asked as she fixed a flower onto her shirt.

"The Rashneeshi laws," he replied.

"What's that?" said Melody.

"Well, when the Bhagwan came to Oregon, thousands of people were camping out to worship, so the state said that no more than 250 people can camp out together anymore."

"Oh," I said, wondering what we should do.

The friendly long-haired guy then seemed to wake up from a standing sleep for a moment, announcing, "Hey, I know a great place you can stay if you want."

"Great," I responded optimistically. "Where is it?"

"Heart Valley," he told us with a glowing smile. "It is a private farm about five miles from here." We could tell that he had a loving connection with the place as the look in his eyes showed that he was reliving memories. "The owner's name is Aeron, and I'm sure he won't mind you staying on his land."

After getting sketchy directions, we drove until we saw a homemade sign for Heart Valley and turned left onto a small dirt road. Upon entering some woods, the bottom of the car started scraping the rutted dirt path, making long gritty noises. We stopped in the darkness, not knowing where to go. There was a small cabin with one light on and a tunnel of trees around the dirt road leading deeper into the woods.

"That way." called a voice in the dark. "There are a few others down in the field," the voice said again, as two people slowly appeared out of the darkness.

"Thanks," I told them.

We drove down through the dark trees and out into a large field. Once out of the trees, we could make out the images of a painted school bus, two minibuses, and a station wagon parked in the field. There was a fire burning with a group of people softly singing to the strum of a Spanish guitar as well as sound of the fire crackling.

After driving across the field, we found a good place to park. Once the car motor died, the silence of nature rose, filling our ears with a soft delight. Our steps seemed loud on the straw-like grass. We walked over toward the circle of people around the fire.

As we approached, warm faces turned toward us. The glow of the small fire speckled their eyes and faces with the flickering colors of yellow and red.

"Hello," I said taking a seat at the circle.

"Hi."

"My name is Clark. This is Chrystal and Melody."

"Hi, good to meet you," replied one of the girls wearing a green and yellow macramé vest. It was quiet for a moment.

"This is a beautiful place," I observed, looking in a full circle around the edge of the large clearing.

"Is this your first time here?" someone else at the fire asked with interest.

"Yeah."

"Believe me, you found the right place," he continued with a look like he knew something very special but wasn't ready to share. "Where are you guys from?"

"Chrystal and Melody are from Seattle. I'm from Tacoma. What about you?" I inquired.

"We are from Canada," answered a girl with a brown cloak and a round face. "They are from New York, and they are from Mexico City," she continued as she pointed out the others around the fire.

"Right on," I replied.

Just before I was ready to ask Chrystal and Melody if they wanted to set up the tent, one of the guys from Mexico City pulled out a joint from under his colorful poncho, lit it, and passed it around the circle. I watched as Chrystal and Melody put their lips to the joint, inhaling deeply.

The group communed together for a while. At one point, I pulled out some dried fruits and vegetables to share with the others.

The evening was amazing, but it was getting late, so I stood up to go put up the tent. Anna, the round-faced girl from Canada, asked, "Mushroom?" extending her hand toward me.

"Sure," I agreed and popped it into my mouth. I had thought that she was offering me more dried food, but the mushroom wasn't dried. I immediately knew that it was more than an ordinary mushroom.

"Don't worry," she assured me with a smile. "It was wrapped up when it was in my vagina while we crossed the border."

I smiled back at her, realizing that setting up the unfamiliar small pup tent that Chrystal brought would become infinitely more interesting. I wasn't even done with the tent when at about three in the morning, Chrystal and Melody came over and helped me finish wrestling the technicolored, shiny material into the form of a shelter. At one point, Melody had to convince me that there really wasn't a little green frog chasing me. Knowing what a simple task it should have been, we all laughed at our efforts, not really caring if it was up correctly or not, just wanting to have a place to get into.

Not bothering to lock the car, we got out a few blankets and sleeping bags, and climbed into the green, crooked tent. I lay in the middle between the two women until Chrystal and I ended up sharing each other's heat but mostly just enjoying the comfortableness of each other's smooth skin until I ended up fully in her sleeping bag. Chrystal and I melted into each other, fully engaged in the beauty of our surroundings and company.

We woke early as the morning sun brightened our tent. I passionately kissed Chrystal on the mouth. Looking into her blue eyes, I ran my fingers through her long blonde hair. Turning around, I kissed Melody on the cheek.

We piled out of the tiny tent together to see that others from the group were already sitting around the fire, sipping coffee.

We joined the group and lazily spoke about the events of the night before. Then we decided that Chrystal, Melody, and I should ride to the fair in. one of the VW buses with the Canadians.

As soon as we arrived, the hippie city was abuzz with people, colors, and sounds. We smoked a joint in the open door of the bus before walking into the circus.

Hours later, I was staring at a group of people naked, but covered in dark mud, rummaging around a little shelter they created within the fairgrounds. A friend whom I had met at a few Grateful Dead shows approached me and announced excitedly, "Om circle in ten minutes."

Broken from my trance, I asked, "Huh?"

"The om circle, man. It is going to happen in ten minutes."

I didn't know what he was talking about, but because he was so excited, I followed him. As we approached the people gathering around the designated area, I found Chrystal and Melody. Everyone was making a giant circle around the entire circular road inside the main fair area. It was so massive that we couldn't see the people on the other side where the circle surrounded wooden buildings and stands.

We joined the hundred-yard-wide circle. As everyone else was doing, I put my right arm around the Deadhead to my right, and Crystal snuggled underneath my left arm with

Melody to her left. We just waited, all packed together with arms tightly around each other when one of the organizers of the Rainbow Gathering came walking by instructing that at exactly 1:00 pm we would all begin to chant "om" in unison.

As the time came, the hundreds of people, all linked together, began to chant "*A-E-I-OUM.*" Although the sound never really became overly loud, the whole area started to reverberate. My entire body began to shake with the resonance. Still slowly chanting "om," I looked at Sam to my right and Chrystal to my left, and we all smiled at the tickling feeling passing through all our bodies. It felt as if the whole group was floating away. We knew that it was a communal feeling that every person in the giant circle was experiencing. When it was over, the sensation continued, and we couldn't believe the power of it. We all felt high from it for hours.

Back at Heart Valley, it was evening. We were sitting around the same fire like we'd done the night before. The group was a bit larger. A man with shoulder-length blondish hair, a multi-colored cotton belt, and knee-high, soft brown moccasins walked up to the fire. Almost everyone recognized him at once. It was Aeron, the owner of Heart Valley.

The people who knew him eagerly asked him questions about how he was and how his day went and about how the Rainbow Gathering was going. Aeron answered politely. Then he pulled out a six-inch American Indian-styled peace pipe. He lit it and ceremoniously passed it around the fire two times. After about an hour he left.

Soon after Aeron returned to the fire. Pulling Melody, Chrystal, and me aside, he asked, "Hey, do you want to come up to the house?"

I really didn't because it was such a great scene at the fire, but Melody and Chrystal both said yes. I picked up the glazed clay drum I had purchased earlier in the day, slung the cotton strap over my shoulder, and we walked through some trees up to the cabin. As we walked in the dark, I could feel Aeron's anticipation for something big, but I didn't know what it was.

As soon as we entered the wooden front door of the cabin, I knew that this was a good decision. There were about fifteen people in the room sitting on the floor in an unfinished circle, and we sat down completing the circle. The floor was wooden with a very large Persian rug covering most of it.

All were relaxed, and most had instruments. I was glad that I had brought my drum. Nothing accidental seemed to be happening. Aeron introduced a few people from the circle, one of whom was North Star, one of four stars in the Rainbow Community hierarchy. North Star had a flute and bowed naturally to us. The verve in the room was tangible.

"There is food in the kitchen for whoever needs it," Aeron told everyone as he stood next to North Star who was sitting on the floor. He then walked over to a wooden cabinet with glass front panels and took out another Native American pipe. This one was about twenty inches long with many beads wrapped around it and two feathers hanging from it.

Like at the fire earlier with the smaller peace pipe, Aeron was ceremonious as he lit the pipe. This time it seemed a more regal action, as if he were a wizard casting a spell. He flawlessly lit a match, held it perfectly to the pipe, and pulled in the smoke before passing it to his right. The room was silent. All eyes were on the large pipe as it moved from mouth to mouth filling the room with aroma. When the pipe got to me, I carefully positioned it on my lips and sucked in hard before passing the pipe on with a small respectful bow of my head to the person to my right.

*Oh, no,* I thought to myself. *That wasn't pot!*

I really didn't know what I was getting myself into. I nervously looked at Chrystal and Melody who also had apprehension in their eyes. They had obviously realized the same thing, and the elevator was going up quickly.

Once the pipe had made it around the entire room, North Star picked up his flute and began to play. Not all at once, but others began to join in on the music. I began rapping on my drum in tune with the group, astounding myself at what was coming out of the instrument in rhythm with the rest of the group. Chrystal grabbed a pair of spoons, and Melody a maraca. We all joined each other in the music, looking around the room at each other, loving the connection, and enjoying the communal music we were making together.

Aeron instigated another circle pass of the same pipe, and when it came to me, with great respect, I turned the long pipe sideways, held it to my forehead signaling that I had reverence for what was happening, but that I wasn't willing to go to another level.

*Maybe it was acid*, I thought to myself. Although the carpet was moving, it was the movement of the objects around the room and behind me that began to take me out of the serene moment. I began to have second thoughts about whether this was a good idea.

*Will I be stuck in this place?* I thought. *Is this eternity?*

A woman stood up, and I watched her walk out of the circle and toward the kitchen. Her movements were stuttered like I was seeing every third frame in a movie. She looked at me curiously as if she were trying to figure out what I was staring at. Her eyes were piercing. I buried my mind back into the drum and again joined the collective until the music began to fade away, and so did I.

The flute stopped.

"Do you see the rainbow?" North Star said.

I heard a few mumbles from others as I followed the swirling rainbow streaking peacefully in the center of the room. It was like the rainbow was following itself. I was dazzled.

I looked over at Chrystal who was also staring at the empty space in the middle of the room with her head cocked to one side. Her blonde hair was flowing over her shoulders as if it was being blown in the wind.

As I turned my attention to others in the room, all were occupied with something or nothing. A few people were still playing instruments, and a few were trying to have conversations, but most were staring. No one had their eyes shut.

It was North Star who again spoke calmly to the group. "Isn't it wonderful," North Star said, "We made it to the gathering."

As he said this, I felt an overwhelming acceptance about whatever was to come. I felt like I was in contact with a universe of minds thinking the same thing as me. I allowed my mind to bathe in a space it had never been to before.

Hours later the circle dispersed, but the room and kitchen were still full of people. I grabbed Chrystal's hand, smiled at Melody, and we all stood up. We floated over to Aeron, and I looked him deeply in the eye and said, "Thank you." He touched my arm and smiled. He hugged Chrystal and Melody. We walked out of the cabin.

On the walk back toward the tent, the three of us had giant smiles. We held hands and walked with our arms around each other, mostly just saying, "Wow." There still weren't words to describe what had happened in the cabin, and the powerful sensation continued.

Upon reaching the tent, Chrystal wanted to stay outside for a while, so Melody and I entered, lay down, and immediately embraced in an extremely tight hug on the floor of the tent. We began kissing. Melody and I were still stuck together when, later, Chrystal entered the tent, lay down, and kissed me firmly on my bare back. The moist kiss sent tingling ripples of love, which started at the place of the kiss and spread, through my whole body.

"Wow," I heard one of them say again as we all fell asleep and slipped into dreams about each other, people we had met, and other travelers we would meet on the road.

## *About You*

*Have you ever had a psychedelic experience so remarkable that you really can't put into words what it was like? What caused it and what do you remember about it?*

*What ways can we have psychedelic experiences without drugs?*

Do Something Extraordinary

*Ask yourself if seeking out a one-time psychedelic experience might be for you, whether it be through meditation, sweat lodge, or other method.*

# TWENTY

# REFLECTIONS ON TRANSCENDENCE

While I appreciate each of the pillars of meaning, I feel a giddy affinity toward transcendence. Like purpose, many of us might think of transcendence as being an all-overwhelming moment that requires a significant ingredient, such as taking drugs or joining an esoteric ritual. However, I don't think this has to be the case. Yes, a transcendental moment can be triggered by a mind-blowing psychedelic experience, but equally it can result from less-orchestrated situations—hearing the perfect song at the right time or, as John Muir highlights, staring up at a great redwood and experiencing its magnificence as "traces of the thoughts of God, and leading on and on into the infinite cosmos."

Reflecting on transcendental moments in my life, I think there are two main categories: post-fear transcendence and awe-inspired transcendence. Although they both fit into what I'd classify as "transcendence," they are significantly different.

Post-fear transcendence occurred for me when I endured cholera in the Sahara Desert and when I suffered the Nigerian guard as he held a gun to my head. In each of these, there existed a shocking reality that I might die, but the transcendental moment wasn't at the peak of the fear. Rather, it came about just following the fear-moment when my understanding of my mortality became acutely real, and awe-inspiring feelings of release and gratitude filled my body. It was as if I could reflect on my life-history and see my infinite future simultaneously. I was able to clearly identify the important from the unimportant in my present.

The second category, awe-inspired transcendence, occurs during moments of awe inspired by something that objectively confronts the senses causing an immediate mental and physiological reaction. In my case, this something has included psychedelically-induced states, like ingesting LSD at an urban Grateful Dead concert and ingesting hallucinogenic concoctions deep in the remote Amazon, but drugs don't always have to be involved. I experienced extremely powerful transcendental moments staring up at the aurora borealis in Alaska or staring into the eyes of a woman while in love.

The trigger of the awe-inspiring moment is less important than the effect. Whether transported by terror, psychic lucidity, or majestic awareness, this kind of transcendence opens us up to a sense of universal clarity where all ordinary things in life become suddenly unimportant and the comforting idea that life and death are both connected to the same existence becomes evident in a tangible fashion.

During a transcendental moment, there is no sense of caring about material possessions or even how to "spend time wisely;" rather, thoughts are distilled to a point where only the self (sometimes with an aura of family and friends) becomes relevant, and the intersection between earthly awareness and boundless eternal existence becomes a conscious circumstance. The result is that all non-meaningful things surrounding our lives become insignificant; we're left with a rare distilled moment of unashamed nakedness in the universe as we stare meaning in the face. This kind of transcendence can lead us to experience a moment as dramatically described by William Shatner in his 1968 record *Transformed Man* where he "touched ... the face ... of God."

Whether driven by a moment of fear, a moment of elation, or simply a moment of awe, the main characteristic of transcendence is that some sort of shift has occurred. We somehow view ourselves and our relationship to others, the universe, or God from a new perspective, which may or may not change the way we choose to live our lives. This shift often comes with a realization that we are but a speck in an infinite universe. The humbling sensation of this surprisingly doesn't foster feelings of despair or meaninglessness; rather, as Esfahani Smith has shown, we are filled with a deep and powerful sense of meaning. I strongly believe this state of universal connectedness can allow us to feel a productive yet ego-less importance as we maneuver our way through life's wonderful joys as well as arduous challenges.

## *About You*

*Can you think of a transcendental moment in your life? How did it affect you, and are you still transformed by it? How do you think you'd react to a transcendental experience in your life now? What could you do to foster a transformative experience or awe-inspiring moment? Natural national monuments, the cosmos, and other extraordinary spaces are waiting for you.*

*If you want to share with me an amazing transcendental experience you've had, please do so. You can reach me at Erik@ErikSeversen.com.*

# PART 4

# STORYTELLING

*[O]ne of the best ways for people to make meaning through storytelling is to reflect on the pivotal moments of their lives ... and consider how those moments shaped who they are and how their lives have unfolded.*

—Emily Esfahani Smith

# TWENTY-ONE

# THE BWI AND THE JAGUAR

*French Guiana, South America. 1992.*
*Twenty-Three Years Old*

*It is not so much a possession of the soul, but rather an infection of the mind*, I thought to myself. *The bwi is only a tool of many, which is used as an instrument for protection from death.*

These thoughts started when I set out on a hike from Maripasula to Papaichton in French Guiana near the northeast border of Brazil. The normal travel between the two villages is by canoe on the Maroni River that separates French Guiana and Suriname, but wanting to see what the land route was like, I decided to load a small pack and set off into the Amazon forest. It should have been a one-day trek, but I felt compelled to leave in the late afternoon, knowing that I would have to stay one night alone in the jungle.

While I had spent time in the bush before and felt well equipped for the findings of the physical world, this trip offered me something more. In this jungle trek, I felt like I was entering a strange new frontier of human and animal spirits long since decayed beneath the red earth and roots. According to both the Aluku Maroons and Wayana Indians, the forest was full of sentient beings beyond just people, animals, and plants. I had listened to many stories about the spirits in the forest. Some of the stories were actually warnings that I had dismissed as tales of the jungle.

One direct warning was told to me by a young man named Yeni, an Aluku born in South America, but originating from West Africa. Like all the Aluku, Yeni descended from Africans brought to French Guiana and Suriname as slaves. However, the slavery narrative ended there as the captives revolted, fleeing into the jungles to maintain their independence. Mostly they hid from the 18th century colonists, but they fought them when they had to.

Looking at me intently one evening, Yeni leaned over and told me, "There is a snake."

"A snake?" I responded curiously.

"He may live in your house, an' you don' know it. You only see him when him want you to," Yeni continued.

I realized that Yeni wasn't talking about the standard anacondas and boa constrictors that I saw occasionally in the jungle or along the riverbanks. Yeni was warning me about magic, about voodoo, or *obea*, as it is known in this area.

I was in the jungle for field research in anthropology. Earlier that day, for some ethnological work, I'd asked the kids in Papaichton their names. I didn't know at the time that the way I was asking suggested I was inquiring about their real names. The Aluku generally keep their "real" names secret, so others aren't able to use magic or cast curses on them. That's what the children had figured I wanted to do when I inquired about their real names.

Frightened, the children went home and told their parents. Next, I became immediately known as the outsider who wanted to cast spells on the children. Yeni was asked to give me the warning.

Yeni continued, "Yes, a snake. They is many … but his name is Papa Gadu."

I knew Papa Gadu to be the most powerful *obea* spirit among the Aluku. I began to ask more questions about Papa Gadu, but Yeni's warning had been given. He turned his head slowly. Eerily he held my stare with the corner of his eyes as he lifted a lit cigarette to his mouth. He inhaled deeply and said nothing else.

It was much later that Naipon, someone whom I had gotten quite close with, wanted to share something with me. Naipon was an Ndyuka from Suriname. Like the Aluku, the Ndyuka are maroons, or culturally African displaced people who survive in the jungles of South America.

Naipon and I were spending a week traveling up the Maroni River in a dugout canoe. We were just upriver from Maripasoula at a village I had never been to before when Naipon stated, "I want to introduce you to my uncle."

"Great," I responded, not knowing at the time that among the Ndyuka *obea* magic is passed down from uncle to nephew. Apparently what Naipon was trying to communicate to me was that he wanted to give me some magic from his family.

"My uncle only lives over there," Naipon explained, as he pointed further upriver into the jungle. "Let's go."

Still not knowing what I was getting into, I walked with Naipon for about a half-hour before arriving at a very small village composed of four huts. There were a few children playing in the village. Although small, it had a nice clearing of short grass.

As we approached, I noticed the central marker found in most villages with its carved and painted figures that were supposed to protect the village from the spirits of the forest. I also noticed other poles, some with feathers, small bones, and trinkets. Naipon asked me to wait outside for a moment while he walked into a hut that featured three large, colorful drums sitting outside of it.

"He's ready," Naipon announced, as he walked out of the hut to stand in front of me. Naipon looked nervous.

As I followed him into the very dark, almost pitch-black small hut, I had to duck under a chicken carcass hanging at the entrance. Inside, trinkets and charms were hanging from the particularly low ceiling. Although they were difficult to see, I felt their presence by their small movements and the occasional sounds they made as they bumped into each other.

With a hand gesture, I was instructed to sit across from Naipon's uncle. Naipon sat to my right. Naipon's uncle was shirtless, and he wore many bracelets and necklaces. There was a woman in the corner. We sat for a few minutes. I didn't really know where to look or if I should say anything, and I began to feel horribly nervous myself.

Finally, the uncle said something. The woman left and returned moments later with a cauldron full of dry grass and objects. Naipon's uncle studied me and began digging through the small black pot taking out various objects and returning them. Repeatedly he selected metal armbands that I knew to be called *bwis*. Some were black and some were silver. The one he chose for me was thick and copper. This was to be put over my bicep as I had seen others wear.

I knew the story: while wearing a *bwi*, a person would be protected from many things. I heard of stories of people being stabbed with knives and not getting harmed. At a funeral ritual, I had even seen dancing possessed men who were wearing *bwis* rake machetes and razor-sharp palm fronds over their bodies. I could see their skin slide back and forth under the pressure of the sharp objects, but no harm came to them.

My heart began to pound when I realized that I was not only witnessing a voodoo ceremony, but that I was the reason for the ceremony. The *bwi* itself isn't known to be protective. It is the spirit that would be linked to it that would possess the wearer at the moment of trouble; thus, supernatural protections would fall into place.

Putting the cauldron aside, Naipon's uncle laid the *bwi* he had chosen on the ground between the three of us. He started talking to himself. The woman in the hut began shaking a rattle and humming. The drums outside at the hut's entrance sounded a fast five-beat rhythm.

As the intensity became palpable, Naipon's uncle's eyes began to roll back. He began shivering and continued to chant. My nervousness became more of a panicking fear as my body felt like it was vibrating. My stomach felt light, and my mind raced.

The chanting became what seemed to be a conversation, but a one-sided conversation. It was as if Naipon's uncle were speaking with someone not there. I didn't understand the language, which didn't even seem to be Ndyuka, but I could hear both my name and the word for "foreigner," mentioned many times. Naipon's uncle's body continued to shake. He continued talking, and it was obvious that I was hearing one half of a dialogue.

Naipon suddenly handed me a five French franc note and asked me to place the money over the *bwi*, which I did. Naipon's uncle then put a few charms over the money, picked up a bottle, and began sprinkling white rum on the money, charms, and *bwi*. As he wildly sprinkled the rum, he began convulsing, sweating profusely, and weeping. He kept talking, and the crying turned to sobbing as he rocked back and forth. This lasted for about five minutes until he began to calm. The woman with the rattle stopped as did the drums outside.

As soon as the chanting, rattle, and drums ceased, the buzzing feeling of my body and head felt even more apparent. I hoped all would be over soon and that my sensations would return to normal.

The four of us in the hut sat as the energy of the room began to relax. I too began to relax with it.

Finally, Naipon's uncle began speaking calmly with Naipon who looked at me and told me that I could take the *bwi*.

During the entire scene, I'd been shaking with anxiety and praying to myself, *Dear Lord Jesus, please be with me. Please don't let anything happen to me that you do not approve of. I accept the material possession of the* bwi, *but I refuse the spirits to enter me.*

I repeated this over and over, and now it was time to take the *bwi.* I reached out and delicately and respectfully picked it from under the money and charms and off the dried grass covering a small patch of the dirt floor.

Naipon and his uncle told me to put it on, which I did.

As I put the *bwi* on, I felt like a warrior—potent, powerful, and elite. As I left the hut, I thanked them many times for the amazing gift with which they had honored me.

It was very bright when Naipon and I exited the hut. We squinted, adjusting to the light as we left the small village the way we had entered. Once back on the trail outside of the village, I asked Naipon, "Why was your uncle crying?"

"He wasn't crying," Naipon casually responded.

This was strange for me to hear since we both had witnessed Naipon's uncle crying hysterically with tears flowing down his face.

In the same casual voice, Naipon explained, "My uncle wasn't crying. It was his *kumanti* spirit possessing him who was crying." He seemed to make no association between the spirit and his uncle's physical body, and he made no explanation for the sobbing.

Reflecting on my time with Naipon and his uncle set an uneasy feeling in me as I left the village for my overnight solo trek in the jungle. Since I had started late in the day, it was getting darker.

As I walked alone along the path between Maripasula and Papaichton, I saw a long streak in the mud—the track from a very large snake. Immediately I thought of Papa Gadu and other stories of zombies and spirits. This left me feeling strangely uneasy.

I reached up and touched the *bwi* that was on my left arm and realized the dangerous position I was putting myself in. I felt that by believing in or even accepting the *bwi*, I was giving the *kumanti* or *kunu* spirits permission to enter. I unconsciously recited a Bible verse from Revelations that I had known from my Sunday school days as a child: *I will stand at the door and knock, if any man hear my voice and open it, I will come into him and sup with him and he with me.*

As I said the verse, I envisioned a scene of God knocking at a large wooden door with a snake loosely coiled at his feet, a large snake, a constrictor, Papa Gadu. The snake was ready to enter the door once it opened.

Then my mind took the form of third person, and I looked onto my body as it shivered under the control of a demon. My heart began to pound. However, it wasn't a spiritual attack that would play out that day.

An ever so slight crack of a twig turned my attention to the noises of the jungle. I then remembered someone commenting that it isn't always what you see in the forest that is frightening, but what you don't see. The imagination is much more powerful than the reality you see in waking life ... sometimes.

I loosened the knife that was at my belt and nervously flipped my machete from my right hand to my left. This trick was not possible in reverse because of the infections that had taken hold of my right hand when I'd cut it along the riverbank hunting for food weeks earlier. After a few awkward slashes with my healthy left hand, I decided that if something unexpected were to happen, I would do better with the machete in my infected right hand.

Provoked by the faint noise and becoming tense with fear, I decided to set up camp. I quickly hung my hammock between trees. Before I started to gather firewood, I began to wonder about that sound I'd heard. *Is my mind playing tricks on me?* I thought as I made a small pile of branches. A howler monkey roared in the distance.

When I focused my energy on starting a fire, I became calmer and more confident. However, it came again—a slight sound somewhere near the jungle floor.

It was quickly getting dark. The sun was gone. My heart began to pound furiously, and I moved hastily. After wasting twelve waterproof matches on tiny, moist twigs, I began to be more afraid. I dug out a pack of cigarettes from my backpack. There were three left, and I tossed the pack by the twigs. Digging deeper into my pack, I found two candles, and that is when I heard it—the unmistakable growl of a cat.

*Please, dear Lord, let that be an ocelot,* I prayed.

I ran two steps over to the twigs and quickly broke up a cigarette, hoping that the tobacco and paper would flame up with the strike of one of my flare matches. It did—for about fifteen seconds—then nothing. Intently, I tried to hold myself still to listen for the direction of the cat.

A low branch moved at the edge of the small clearing. In desperation, I shakily lit one of my last matches, ignited one of the small candles, and stuck it under the pile of tobacco, cigarette paper, and a few small twigs. The small light heisted until I bowed down on my hands and knees and gently blew.

It was then that our eyes met—it was a jaguar.

My chest and stomach rose from anxiety to panic. I felt like my body was floating away. Shaking, it was difficult not to blow too hard and extinguish the growing flame. I groped around the leaves behind me, searching for my machete.

I decided that if the jaguar was to charge, I would attempt to use my pack as a shield and chop with all my might toward the head of the jaguar, knowing that if I did not succeed the first time, it would probably mean death. Once the smooth cat had its claws hooked firmly into my flesh, it would aim for the neck attempting to sever life from between the head and the body. The powerful jaws would not relax until all was still.

The crouching jaguar turned its head slowly, and the moon reflected off each eye, first the left then the right. As I bent toward the young fire, I felt the pressure of the *bwi* as if it were gripping my upper left arm. Not intending to take my eyes off the large animal, I noticed that the jaguar had turned around and was now standing with his buttocks toward the camp and his tail up. The jaguar's furry white testicles boldly protruded from between his legs. It seemed he was presenting a symbol of his superiority before he faded back into the forest.

## *About You*

*Have you ever been petrified by something that almost paralyzed you with fear? What happened and did it change the way you think about anything?*

*What do you think are some things that people fear the most and why?*

*Do Something Extraordinary*

*Put yourself in a non-dangerous position where you feel fear or anxiety. This could be sitting alone in a dark room, bungee jumping, or deciding to start a conversation with a stranger at a coffee shop. Be creative to find something that would genuinely frighten you, but something that you could work through without real harm. Tell someone in detail about how you handled your fear.*

# TWENTY-TWO

## NEVER GIVE UP

*Washington State, USA. Eighteen to Twenty-One Years Old*

After graduating from high school, I wanted to go to UCLA in the fall, but my grades in the first two years of high school weren't great. As an optimist, I thought I could get in, and this is what I told Mrs. Elbert during my senior year counseling appointment.

Mrs. Elbert's response: she leaned forward, pushed herself away from the desk, and told me that I'd *never* get into a school like that. That was all she had to say, and she walked out of the room, leaving me alone with the weight of her response.

I applied anyway and was not accepted. So, I left for Europe with almost no money and no plans at all. When I got back 2.5 months later, I called my best friend Kirk.

"Kirk, what are you going to do this fall?"

"I'm going to go to Green River," Kirk responded.

"Okay, me too," I decided.

Next, I called Green River Community College for an application.

Since GRCC was near my grandmother's house in Kent, Washington, I lived with her. My grandmother and I made a great team. I think we loved the routine we created while I was living there. Both of us had breakfast together each day: one piece of toast with homemade raspberry jam, one soft-boiled egg, and half of a grapefruit. An average school day was me feeding the cows and chopping wood for about 45 minutes in the morning, spending most of the day on campus, and returning for dinner, which almost always included some form of home-grown beef and potatoes.

After dinner, I'd study until *Wheel of Fortune* came on. This was my 80-year-old grandmother's favorite show. I'd watch with her, so she had someone to be proud with when she guessed the hidden phrases before the contestants, and she almost always did.

After *Wheel of Fortune*, she'd put on Lawrence Welk while knitting. I'd go back to studying at the dining room table but still in earshot of the easy music. As long as she'd finished her daily crossword puzzle, Grandma would usually go to bed around nine. I'd continue studying until exactly midnight when I'd walk down the steep hill to Meridian Lake. I'd grab our red canoe from next to the pump house and slide it into the water. I'd get in and take two or three powerful strokes toward the center of the lake with the wooden paddle. Then I'd lie down in the center of the canoe looking up at the clouds when it was overcast or at the stars when they were out. I'd float for about fifteen minutes. Lying still, looking up as the water lapped the sides of the boat was an amazing and refreshing way to quiet my mind at the end of every day.

I enjoyed my routine at GRCC too. When I decided I wanted to take more classes than normal, so I could take a quarter off to travel to Africa, my routine became almost fanatical. An average student class load was 13 to 15 credits, but I didn't want to fall behind my peers, so I tried to sign up for double the number of courses. I was told that I couldn't because the administrators thought my grades would suffer. I pushed, and they said they'd have to get permission from the dean. I was later told that the discussion with the dean was quite comical. Evidently, it started with his review of my transcript and GPA up to that point and ended with a few behind-the-scenes stories about me.

The first story was how some teachers came to him to ask about a policy regarding students wearing shoes. As I was a bourgeoning throwback hippie at the time when I began GRCC, I wore only a white t-shirt and jeans for the first month of school. For the first week, I didn't wear any shoes either, so the teachers asked about the policy. The dean said that he didn't know about anything written but suggested they ask me to wear shoes and see how I'd respond. Evidently there was a bit of anticipation about how I would react. They thought that I might try to fight on principle or something. When one of the teachers asked if I would wear shoes, I simply said, "Okay." I wore a pair of Birkenstocks, and it never came up again.

The second story they floated about me involved the Intro to Western Philosophy professor. Apparently, he didn't like me very much. During the first half of the quarter, I thought our (meaning, between him and me) class discussions and differing viewpoints were healthy philosophical dialogue. I finally realized that the professor didn't like the playful debating. I only corrected him a few times and in small ways. One time was when he was using one of Plato's examples for his Theory of Forms from *The Republic*. During an explanation of Plato's three types of Forms, the professor cited one as the "chair." I reflexively interjected, "The bed." The professor argued the point for a minute, and I let it go, but I know he checked after class, as I did, and saw that I'd been right.

The class was made up of about thirty students many of whom weren't very engaged. The front of the room was occupied by the more engaged students. I sat in the front row next to two girls whom I chatted with often. After reading Plato's *The Republic*, Sartre's *Nausea* and some other book, which I had also previously read, the two came up to me in the hallway after class and admitted that they were petrified of the midterm, which was to be five in-class essay responses.

To help I told them that I could meet them for lunch and discuss the class with them over a few days before the exam. Over our lunch sessions they were very vocal about expressing their appreciation for some of the ideas I extracted from the readings. Then we took the test. They both received As. I got a C—and I was furious.

At the end of the quarter, the final was made up of a term paper about Robert Persig's *Zen and the Art of Motorcycle Maintenance*, Plato and Aristotle, and Classical and Romantic ways of thought. I worked arduously on the paper, which turned out to be over seven pages longer than the minimum ten pages required. I meticulously double-checked the evidence for my ideas and the relationships I'd made in the paper. As we handed the papers in, I deliberately waited to be the last to turn mine in. As my professor sat looking up at me from his desk, I calmly stated, "I'm confident you'll like it, and if you don't, I might have to ask the dean his opinion about it."

Though from then on, the instructor wouldn't look me in the eye while passing me in the hallway, I got an A in the class ...

The dean agreed that I could take seven classes equaling twenty-seven credits during the spring quarter. It was exhilarating. I had daily classes pretty much from 8 am to 5 pm with a few gaps during which I'd study. When I did get home, I'd study until exactly midnight and start again at 6 am before school. The breakfast, chopping wood, dinner, and watching a bit of TV with Grandma remained. I would study pretty much all day both Saturday and Sunday.

Only once a week on either Friday or Saturday night, I would hang out with friends. We'd usually meet at one of our houses or apartments. From time to time, we had really fun parties. There was one occasion when Grandma's poor hearing did come in handy. Sometimes we'd have ten or fifteen people drinking beer and liquor, raucously chatting, and laughing hysterically at jokes in Grandma's living room until 2 am, and she'd be sleeping in the next room. As long as she kept her hearing aid out, and we cleaned up well, it worked out well for everyone.

It really was a great group of friends I made at the community college. There was Gladys and her brother Neil, Vishu, also known as Ting, Willy, Don, Fred, Sophie, Sun, Stacy, and a few others. We were a diverse group of students, all excited about learning and pursuing our dreams, and we would certainly laugh a lot. It wasn't until I got back from Africa and had known them for over a year that we really became close. We loved each other and became like a wonderful family. Although excited, I knew I'd miss them when Green River hired me to travel to Japan to help set up a branch campus in a town called Kanuma.

In the end, I think my time living with my Grandma and going to Green River couldn't have been much better. Between the time on my Grandma's farm, the amazing friends I met, the incredible education I received, and spending 4.5 months in Asia, I grew a lot during that time.

When the time came, I applied to UCLA again. With the editorial help of my English teacher, I wrote an application essay to UCLA. In this essay, I explained that I thought I was ready for the University of California—and UCLA agreed. The next chapter of my education—and really, my life— would begin in Los Angeles.

## *About You*

*Have you ever overcome something that others thought was impossible or accomplished something that you are very proud of? What was it and how did you feel when you overcame the odds and did it?*

*What are some of the most important things to keep in mind while working toward a lofty goal?*

*Do Something Extraordinary*

*Do you know of anyone who is currently in a discouraging situation where they are struggling with how, or whether, to continue? If you think the pursuit of their goal is positive, encourage them not to give up. Be a motivating force. If you are in a discouraging situation, remind yourself why you started and make a list of reasons why you shouldn't give up.*

# TWENTY-THREE

# SURFING

*USA, Costa Rica, Jamaica, Australia. 2008–2015*

After about eight years in Los Angeles, I confessed to my good friend Wil, "I love LA, but I'm starting to feel a bit claustrophobic—the people, the traffic. I'm thinking about moving somewhere with more space."

Wil immediately understood how I felt, but he didn't encourage me to follow my quest for a more rural area in order to connect with nature. Rather, he simply informed me, "I'm going to come by your house tomorrow at six in the morning, and we are going to go surfing. If you aren't up, I'm going to break down your door and drag you out of bed."

I knew Wil well. We had met many years earlier at a boxing match in Virginia. Wil was an intense guy, and I seriously believed that if I wasn't up, he would break down my door and drag me out of bed.

The next morning I was up and ready, sipping coffee on my porch. At 6 am sharp, Wil pulled up in a classic 1950s Chevy Bel Air with two surfboards strapped to the roof.

"You ready?" Wil asked as he got out of the car and shook my hand.

"Yep," I confirmed, still tired and a bit cold in the morning air.

We first drove down to El Porto to check the waves and then decided on a lesser-surfed area near the El Segundo jetty. We parked at a lot at the end of Grand Ave and walked with the boards about a quarter mile to the south side of the jetty. Wil's board was a fiberglass ten-foot custom. He brought a 9.5-foot yellow soft top for me. Wil called it "the log."

After teaching me a few basics, Wil left me alone to figure it out. Wil was smart to take me away from all the people he knew at El Porto because I mostly fumbled and thrashed around on the board, looking exactly like the kook I was. Finally, I went for a three-foot wave. It wasn't pretty, but I managed to stand for probably two seconds. It was amazing. I was hooked.

When I paddled back out, a seal popped its head up and looked at me from about five feet away. It was a sign. Although I was only four miles from my house and two hundred feet into the ocean, I felt like I was a thousand miles from LA. I was *in* nature. No longer was I interested in moving anywhere.

We surfed for a bit and then had breakfast at Wendy's Cafe in El Segundo. It felt cool sitting at Wendy's with my board shorts and wet hair along with all the other real surfers in the place.

When I arrived at work at 9:00 am, I felt like I had been on vacation for a week.

In my early days of learning, Wil and I would go back and forth between El Porto and the jetty. My first notable wave: a rogue wave, larger than the others. It was still only about shoulder-high, but to me it was enormous. I paddled into it. It looked like a closeout wave, meaning one that leaves no escapable angle to surf and instead crushes everything in its path. As soon as the wave crashed, Wil was a bit concerned. His concern doubled when he didn't see me and my board pop up in the soup of whitewater near the sand. He didn't see me there because somehow, miraculously I actually caught the wave and rode it about two hundred feet along the beach, almost all the way to the jetty.

Eventually Wil started bringing me surfing with some of his surfing brothers. There was Matthew, who had long blond hair and was halfway to the Spicole stereotype from *Fast Times at Ridgemont High*. Matthew was an interesting cat, and I had him entered in my phone as "Surfer Dude." In addition to surfing, he was also a skydiving instructor.

At the parachuting school where Matthew worked, there was a circular, aboveground swimming pool that was five feet deep. One day while Matthew was jumping out of an airplane, he noticed some people swimming in the pool below. He thought it would be funny to swoop down, pull on the parachute uplift cords right before the pool, pop up, and land in the water.

It didn't work as well as he thought though. When he was skimming near the ground at about twenty miles per hour, nothing happened when he pulled the cords. Matthew ended up plowing right into the side of the pool. All the moms and kids in yellow rubber inner tubes ended up flowing out of the collapsing pool and sliding, with all the water, onto the grass—along with Surfer Dude and his parachute.

I love this story about Matthew because it reminds me that I'm not the only one who likes to try ridiculous things, even if they don't always work.

Matthew was also a dolphin magnet. He said it was because one of his boards had a small dolphin painted on it. With Matthew, we'd often see dolphins, and I always loved it, especially when they would get right up next to us within a few feet. Sometimes they would tilt as they swam by and look me right in the eye. It was close enough eye contact that I wondered what the dolphins were thinking. I had a weird impression that the dolphins were wondering the same about me. In the ocean, these amazing animals seemed like our friends, and sometimes, they'd even ride the waves right along with us.

At this point, I'd been surfing with Wil and others for about six weeks. I even had my own board—a beautiful, refurbished 9.5-foot Becker created by one of the original Becker shapers. I was stoked that I found a great board without paying a ton. I was still wearing the wetsuit that Wil had given me on the first day we'd gone out.

One day, we paddled out at El Porto and caught a few waves. We'd been in the water for a while and were sitting on our boards waiting for the next set. It was a cool winter morning. The water felt ice-cold, and I was freezing.

"Aren't you cold?" Surfer Dude asked as he looked over at me.

"Aren't we all?" I replied.

"No, we're fine," Surfer Dude responded, starting to laugh. "Look," he called to the others, "I can see his tattoo through the wetsuit."

Everyone was cracking up. That's when I realized why I was the only one with blue lips. It was an awesome gesture for Wil to give me a wetsuit, but it was so old and worn that most of the rubber had flaked off, rendering it almost useless against the cold. That day, I went to ET Surfboards and got a 3/2 Body Glove that actually worked. The next morning it felt fantastic in the water. I even caught a few good waves.

Surfing to me isn't just about standing on a board. It is much more. It is about the comradery of checking waves with the people I'm surfing with. It's about watching out for each other in the surf. It's about the beautiful beaches and places that you find while looking for the perfect wave. It is also the out-of-the-ordinary things that can happen.

I wanted to surf the famous Hatteras Beach in the Outer Banks of North Carolina. This beach is one of the professional Surfing World Championship locations. I didn't know anything about Hatteras other than its famous name in surfing. I rented a board and hired a surf-guide to go with me. After catching a few waves, we were peacefully sitting on the outside of the breakers, resting and talking, when about two hundred fish from about three inches long to about eighteen inches long jumped out of the water around us. It was bizarre to be right in the middle of this.

"Cool," I remarked, as I looked at the guide. His eyes were huge. He didn't appear to find it as cool as I did.

"Something is down there," he warned as he flattened himself on his board and quickly began paddling toward shore. He was avoiding being a shark's next meal. It could have been a dolphin, but we didn't see one pop up for air. I quickly followed his lead. This is an instance of one of those out-of-the-ordinary things that happened due to surfing.

I fell in love with the idea of surfing in Tamarindo, Costa Rica, while watching Bruce Brown's amazing classic movie *Endless Summer*. In this film Mike Hynson and Robert August circumvent the world, switching hemispheres to remain in summer for a full year and to surf.

My wife and I visited Costa Rica together. We rented a jeep and explored the mountains and jungles. Then it was on to the beaches—and Tamarindo.

I rented a board, which looked great on top of the jeep, but it was the surfing that made it really great. As in Hatteras, I asked the guy I rented the board from, Retta, if I could hire a guide just for a bit to show me any dangerous currents, reefs, or local areas to avoid.

Without even thinking about it, Retta told me, "Yeah, I'll go with you. The waves are going to be good tomorrow at 5 am, so you don't have to pay me. I'll be out there anyway."

At five in the morning, I met Retta at his shop across from the beach. Retta was short and very skinny with very dark skin, long black hair, and a look about him that suggested he didn't worry about much in life. We walked down just south of where a river was running into the ocean. There was a small crowd in the lineup.

The beach was beautiful with a perfectly sandy bottom and warm, clear water. As soon as we paddled out, Retta announced to the other surfers, "Guys, it's okay, he's with me. His name's Erik." They all casually nodded.

Retta and I sat through a few sets, and then he called out, "Hey, guys, let Erik get this one!" They all agreed.

At this point, I still wasn't a very good surfer (and I'm still not), so for the first few times, Retta hopped off his board in the 4.5-foot water and pushed me into the wave. I sailed beautifully on the glassy blue wave, riding it all the way to the beach. I immediately paddled back out.

As soon as I reached the lineup, another set was coming through. Retta hollered again, "Hey, guys, let Erik get this one." He gave the "hang-loose" or shaka sign to them. They all shaka-ed back in agreement. Retta then immediately pushed me into another wave.

After another great ride, I paddled out again. As soon as I reached the lineup, Retta did it again: "Hey, guys, let Erik get this one." They had no problem. They were some of the nicest hard-core locals that I'd ever met. Of course, it was only because I was with Retta.

Because of their generosity in giving me waves, after forty minutes of catching wave after wave and paddling back out each time, I was absolutely exhausted. I had to almost argue with Retta that I really didn't want the next wave, and it was wonderful.

Another noteworthy wave experienced was at San Onofre, California, when I was with Surfer Dude. We left early in the morning and drove down from LA. We started on the bluffs high up and watched the ripples in the water below the cliff. All I saw was a bunch of lines moving in a parallel pattern toward the beach, but Matthew could see much more. "They are going to be big today," he observed.

We decided to go down to Churches Beach. Just getting to the outside past the surf zone was difficult for me with the powerful waves trying to push me back to the beach even though I was using the closest thing to a channel there was. Once outside the breaking waves, it was beautiful.

A large set began to come through, and as the third wave of the set was approaching, Matthew called out, "Let's take it!"

I still wasn't a very confident surfer, and it was by far the largest wave I'd attempted. However, rather than closing my eyes and praying as my scared self was telling me to do, I pointed the board toward the beach and paddled without looking back. And it worked.

The drop of the wave was smooth and long, and I headed left along the beach. Since I was goofy-footed with my right foot forward, I faced the wave rather than facing the direction it was carrying me. I felt more comfortable like that. It was an amazingly long wave. I was crouching and awkwardly turning back and forth on the face of the wave. Matthew just calmly glided in a relaxed upright stance a few feet away from me. He yelled, "Party wave!"

Another outstanding wave, the Jamaica wave, was entirely different. The west side of Jamaica is by far the most touristy with the groomed beaches and all-inclusive resorts. The good surf-worthy waves are on the distant east coast. With my family in tow, we drove over to the remote Boston Bay.

It didn't take long to find a surfboard to rent at the beach, but the only option was a reggae-themed red, green, and yellow board. It was totally beat-up and cracked with duct tape helping to hold it together. I didn't really mind. I just wanted something to use.

I got advice to stay along the left side of the bay along the rock cliff, and the water would naturally pull me toward the opening of the bay where the breakers were. The tall, skinny guy with long dreadlocks also told me to avoid walking on any rocks because of the spiky sea urchins and that the reef where the waves would break was pretty shallow.

The "paddle out" was the easiest of my life. I just floated on the waterlogged board as the current calmly took me out toward the waves along the rocky cliffs. When I looked back, I noticed that my family and all the Rastafarians were watching me. I didn't know it then, but I'd bet a hundred bucks now that the Jamaicans were secretly taking bets on what was going to happen to me.

I was about two hundred yards out. I waved as I got near the edge of the bay. They all enthusiastically waved back. I was definitely the main attraction of the day.

When I reached where the waves were breaking, I paddled toward the center of the bay. I wasn't tired because I hadn't needed to paddle far. A big set began to roll in. I went over the first wave before it broke, and its great height surprised me. Frankly, it frightened me. The second wave was much the same, but I decided to go for the third. As soon as the second wave had passed, the third was upon me, so I flattened myself on the board, glanced back, and paddled with all my might—but something was wrong.

In every wave I'd ever been on, when I'd paddle, even if I missed the wave, I would be paddling toward shore, but not this time. Because of the massiveness of the wave hitting the shallow reef, it was sucking me backwards toward the ocean into the face of the wave. It was a car wreck of a crash as I toppled off the top of the wave and into the water. Thank God, I didn't slam end-over-end onto the shallow reef, but I didn't have any time to think.

The fourth wave of the set was right behind me, so I just scrambled to get the board pointed toward the shore. I paddled as hard as I could, and the wave crashed right on top of me. Somehow, I stayed on the board, still lying down. Although it was only a washing-machine of whitewater jetting me toward to beach, I stood up and rode it all the way in.

It was an inglorious and awkward attempt at what anyone would call real surfing, but evidently, I had done better than some of the unsuspecting amateur surfers who ended up at Boston Bay. All the local Rastas were cheering when I stepped out of the water.

My shin was bleeding from something, and the water on my wet skin made it look even more dramatic, but all were cheering with me. One of the guys offered me a puff from a lit celebration joint, which I politely refused. I was only on the face of one wave, and even though I played around in the whitewater inside the bay for a bit, it was definitely enough for me. I was absolutely stoked to be there.

One of the Rastas who must have only been about sixteen then took the board, went out, and flawlessly lit up one of the outside waves. When he came back to the beach, I gave him a surf magazine, knowing that he was probably as good as some of the people in it with absolutely no real gear at all.

In time, I actually ended up in a surfing tournament. It was in Australia just north of Manly Beach near Sydney. I started surfing next to an Australian guy and a young woman he was teaching. I was aware that the current was pulling me further from them, but the waves were still great. There were other surfers all along the beach, so I didn't mind too much.

It wasn't long before I caught my wave of the day. It was a fast right, and it seemed to go on and on. I was sailing along it happily when I passed two guys sitting on their boards. They were yelling loudly, and I enjoyed hearing their words of encouragement even though with their strong Aussie accents and my vivid attention to the wave I really didn't hear what they were saying. I loved their emphatic excitement over my awesome wave.

Right before I fell off the wave I heard the loud blow-horn sound, and I realized that I had missed the markers on the beach that were blocking off a section of the ocean for the surf competition. I knew a tournament was going on because the guy I rented the board from had told me, but I certainly had no intention of joining it. A guy on a megaphone standing on the beach near some tables made it abundantly clear that I wouldn't receive a trophy. He was also very clear with a few expletives that I should get the hell out of the way.

Whenever I get interested in something, I usually go all out, and the same was true for surfing. I signed up for both *Surfer* and *Surfing* magazines, and I read as many books on surfing as I could find. From technique to musings, I read it all. It was in one of the books that I realized why surfing had affected me so profoundly. It was a book called *West of Jesus,* and it had nothing to do with organized religion.

Basically, the first part of *West of Jesus* is about adrenalin junkies and what skydivers, rock climbers, etc., get from the search for the thrill. The second part of the book is about meditation, yoga, gurus, and what these peaceful individuals get out of what they do. The third part speaks about the size of waves and how micro waves are too big, gamma waves are too small, but the ocean wave is the only tangible wave at a scale that humans can recreationally enjoy. Then the book comes together at the end and explains how surfing offers all three elements: the thrill, the deep peace, and the ocean wave.

While surfing, you get the adrenalin rush of dropping into the face of a wave, but once on the wave, there is a sustained period of meditation as you ride it. This contrast offers an amazing experience. It is an extreme yin/yang in the same activity that offers an overwhelmingly beautiful sensation, especially when you can experience it on a remote island in Indonesia or thirteen minutes from an average neighborhood in Los Angeles.

## *About You*

*Do you have an activity or hobby that you're totally passionate about? What is it and why do you enjoy it so much?*

*Why are activities and hobbies important to people? Do you know anyone who has grown or positively changed due to their engagement with a new activity or hobby?*

*Do Something Extraordinary*

*What is your favorite activity or hobby? Think of a friend who would probably love this activity if they were exposed to it and tell them why they should give it a try. Also, think of an activity or hobby that a friend of yours is passionate about and ask if they'll help you give it a try.*

## *BONUS CHALLENGE*

*As shown by Tim Ferriss and others, pretty much all billionaires and other super successful people claim that daily exercise is a big part of providing them enough energy to fulfill the demands required for peak performance. I challenge you to get more oxygen. If you don't exercise regularly, you should start right away.*

*If you really don't want to exercise, the next best thing is to breathe deeply. We simply don't breathe deeply enough. I challenge you to take three giant breaths, holding each one for several seconds, every two hours throughout the day. You will immediately feel positive effects and more energy. Try it!*

*If you are the type of person who loves challenges, go to www.ErikSeversen.com and check out the EXTRAORDINARY HABITS CHALLENGE. It's certain to help you take your extraordinary to the next level!*

# TWENTY-FOUR

## PARTING WITH PARIS

*Paris, France. 1994 and Now*

Having traveled to over eighty countries in the world and forty-nine of the fifty states in the USA, and having lived for at least three months in five countries and four different states, it is difficult to narrow down the best time-period of my life. Growing up in Washington, studying at UCLA, pursuing graduate studies on the East Coast, and working in Alaska, France, Japan, and Thailand all come to mind as exciting periods of my life, so choosing a best is impossible. What is easy, though, is naming my favorite city. It is Paris.

I'd been to Paris a few times before I moved there when I was twenty-four years old, and I loved becoming part of this amazing city. I almost always dressed nicely while in France. I even had my favorite Parisian costume: khaki pants, black belt, a horizontally thin-striped blue and white shirt, and a red bandana loosely tied around my neck. I loosely modeled myself after Irving in the 1953 Audrey Hepburn film *Roman Holiday*. I felt very French wearing that particular outfit. In the evening, I would also wear a gray blazer, which I thought looked cool casually hanging over the back of the small woven chairs next to tiny round sidewalk tables.

One of the reasons I like Paris so much is because of the myth of Paris—Left Bank cafés, philosophy and art, red velvet jazz clubs, and a unique history of high society gentry as well as bohemian nonconformists. Of course, there exists a drab reality of sometimes gray weather, arrogant denizens, and sidewalks filled with poodle droppings, but I believe the myth of Paris is alive for anyone willing to embrace the city. I wholeheartedly embraced Paris.

There are many things I love about the city from the *haute* fashion Samaritaine billboards along the Champs-Élysées to the used books for sale along the Seine's Left Bank in Saint-Germaine to the artists and painters near Sacré Coeur in Montmartre and even the *facile* metro system with its Gothic signposts.

While living in Paris, I also liked my simple routine of buying cigarettes at the corner *tabac*, purchasing my demi-baguette from the same woman at the *boulangerie* every day, taking the train to Rambouillet in the countryside on Sundays, and enjoying four-hour lunches with Monsieur Beauvoir, his family, and other invited poets, intellectuals, and philosophers.

One of the things I liked best was the ambiguous passage of time and the unhurried conversations with friends at parks or in cafés. Yes, indeed, this was a very important part of my time in Paris.

The day I was leaving Paris was a markedly sad one, but also a full one. I didn't plan it this way, but I ended up making consecutive rendezvous with four different friends for an hour each at Le Départ Café in Saint-Michel. It was a great way to say goodbye individually to some of the people whom I had become closest with during my time there. When it was time to go, Sandrine, my only friend with a car, offered to drive me to the airport. A few other friends wanted to see me off as well, so on top of my large suitcase, we loaded Sofiane, William, Julie, Suzanne, and Sabine into the tiny car. The overloaded compact car could barely make the speed limit as we drove toward Orly Airport.

Being packed tight with six of my closest Parisian friends made it a very special departure. As I walked away from the car, I already longed for the time I'd be back.

Now, as I write this, 23 years later, I can still feel the warmth of my friends in the car as we drove out of Paris. I can see the fogged-up windows. I can feel the moisture in the car and the weight of Suzanne and Sabine on my lap. I can hear their voices. Sofiane is laughing. I can even see their teared-up faces from when I left. I kissed them all many times, it wasn't enough, but my plane was leaving ...

I decided to end this collection of narratives with Paris because living there does seem to be a uniquely special period in my life. Even though it wasn't the most dangerous or the most funny or even the happiest period, it still stands out as a pinnacle of my adventures, encompassing a bit of each of those elements as well as helping shape me as an individual. Hemingway once wrote, "If you are lucky enough to have lived in Paris as a young man, then wherever you go for the rest of your life, it stays with you, for Paris is a moveable feast." I feel so lucky, indeed, to have lived in

Paris, and I certainly agree with Hemingway that Paris stays with a person. I'm delighted that many other places stayed with me as well.

In the end, I found meaning in Paris, but I didn't know it at the time. As with all the places I visited, the meaning wasn't in the physical stone streets and stunning architecture. The meaning wasn't in my friendship with Sofiane or my love for Sabine or something someone said. The meaning wasn't in my physical power as I scared away a mugger with a knife or in my intellect while connecting with a philosophical book. Rather, the meaning was as simple as looking around a hidden corner behind Sacré Coeur, peeking into the office of a famous existential philosopher, and taking the metro down a line I'd never been on before. The meaning, however, wasn't *in* those things, but exists in the relationship I had with all these experiences and how they became part of my being, as majestic buildings provoked awe and as Sofiane and Sabine stirred belonging within me.

Although I didn't recognize it at the time, meaning was everywhere. The reality of walking down a charming cobblestone alley holding a beautiful woman's hand was nothing more than a pleasant moment in between having looked around one corner and looking around the next corner. Would the next corner be a deeper exploration into feelings of love or the discovery of a hidden back entrance into Notre Dame? Would we continue around the next corner together, or would we each turn in different directions? Acting as a spectator, as I watch myself walking down the street, I see infinite possible realities laid before me, and I see the meaning of life unfolding with each step and with each turn.

I find the meaning of life, for me, to simply be the excitement of looking around the next corner and embracing whatever is to come. No experience is necessary for this, just the willingness to step toward it and peek around. Who knows where it will end? And the journey is beautiful ... Endless earthly and heavenly spaces await with quiet exhortations.

## About You

*What was the most meaningful time period in your life? Why was it so special?*

*What are some ways people can find meaning by looking at the past?*

*Do Something Extraordinary*

*Make a list of the distinct time periods of your life. For each time period, write what was meaningful about it and choose a few of these to share with someone close to you.*

# TWENTY-FIVE

# REFLECTIONS ON STORYTELLING

As I reflect on storytelling, my book is almost complete—and so am I. My journey took an ordinary kid from Parkland, Washington, to many distant corners of the world, but I realize that it is the relationships with people that allow me to find what I am looking for. As I've become more and more aware of how much these extraordinary relationships benefit both myself and others, I organically have begun to feel a comfortable satisfaction with my life.

During my study of the world and myself, I've come to see how important belonging has become to me; how personal goals, however lofty, don't provide purpose, but only while working toward things larger than myself, do I enjoy the ultimate satisfaction that comes with seeing my efforts help others.

As I grow in my knowledge of self, I've begun to peer into the wisdom I've realized during transcendental moments. I've asked myself what these moments mean for my tiny existence within a vast universe. I've accepted my humble position while being filled with gratitude for my connectedness with people, God, and the universe.

Through years of travel and meeting people, I've slowly been building an edifice, but it's not quite complete. Like the other pillars of meaning, I cannot raise the last one—storytelling—on my own. Rather, building the final pillar of storytelling requires something more, and it is here that you, the reader, have helped me fully erect the final pillar of my structure. By allowing me to tell my story, the fourth pillar is complete. The roof of meaning in my life has been secured.

I'm humbled and honored that I've been able to share a few of my life's adventures with you. It is my hope that you have received something from my story that will contribute toward your finding greater meaning and satisfaction in your life as well.

As I've stated before, extraordinary people, opportunities, and places are waiting for you. Whether during your next day at work or on an around-the-world expedition, I hope that you recognize the meaning surrounding you. If you are in a positive place in life, I hope that you enjoy seeing how meaning is shaping your experience. If you are searching for something more, I hope you take action toward constructing meaning in your life. The four pillars are an easy place to start, but whatever you do, don't wait for meaning to find you. Go out and grab it.

Reaching out to others, loving, connecting to something larger than yourself, and telling your story can provide you with deep personal meaning, satisfaction, joy, and success beyond your wildest dreams. By doing these simple things, you can choose to live an extraordinary life.

## *About You*

To whom could you reach out to tell your story? Everyone has a unique life that is their story, and there are people who want to hear yours. Is there a spouse, friend, or social group that you could share with? Why don't you build a website, start a blog about yourself, record a video, or write a book? What small step could you take to get your unique story told? Extraordinary listeners are waiting for you.

Everyone has a story. I would love to hear yours. If you have a moment or a time period from your life that you'd like to share, I'd love to hear from you: Erik@ErikSeversen.com.

# TWENTY-SIX

# NOW WHAT?

Recalling my time traveling and meeting people feels wonderful. Recording these memories and experiences has allowed me to revive the moments. This is what I've been doing for the past two years—re-living some of my most memorable experiences of places and people from around the world that made an impact on me. My urge to tell a story was to document what I think is a unique, well-lived life led by an average person who decided not to accept all social norms and restrictive boundaries. It has been a fun journey, and I thank God for each of the extraordinary moments that I've experienced. I appreciate both the good and the bad for forming exactly who I am today.

Even though there are still more stories to tell, it is time to move on and quit looking back. It is time to begin looking forward to the next years and the next adventures that will come. Some of them have already begun. I have some things in mind: several new countries I'd like to see, many people I look forward to meeting, and some tall mountains to climb. However, I realize that these simple goals are nothing but excuses to build upon the pillars of meaning already around me that continually fuel my motivation to assist people and revel in the satisfaction that comes from helping others achieve extraordinary things in their lives.

That is where I want to begin because I find the happiest and most successful moments of my life are when I'm focusing not on myself but on others. As Zig Ziglar famously put it, "You can have anything you want in life, if you just help enough other people get what they want." Like Emily Esfahani Smith, old Zig figured out that a major theme in finding meaning lies in being other-centered rather than self-centered. And that makes all the difference.

# ACKNOWLEDGMENTS

There are many to whom I'd like to say thank you. First, I thank God for my wonderful life. I thank my parents for all they did for me and for allowing me to test the limits of what is possible when I was younger. They didn't let me roam free without boundaries, but they allowed me a lot of freedom to explore. I thank my brother and sister for the love and friendship they showed me over the years. Following about four years in age behind their example was one of the things that encouraged me to push the boundaries. I thank my amazing wife for her love and support, particularly since my adventures and sometimes recklessness didn't end at marriage. With grace she's tolerated my occasional adolescent actions and time away. I thank my two young boys for making me want to continue to discover the world with youthful enthusiasm. I thank Emily Esfahani Smith for her amazing creation, *The Power of Meaning*, which greatly influenced the structure of this book. I thank Nancy Pile for her extraordinary editing skills and insights. She was a delight to work with, and her contributions greatly improved my manuscript. I thank Michael Bowen, Carl Kellogg, Greg Cerbana, and Kirk Rau their comments on early drafts of the narratives. I thank all the many people found in the pages of the narratives. For those whom I loved, I became friends with, or even those I barely knew, you are part of my history. I'm glad that our paths crossed, and I have very fond memories of meaningful moments shared with you. Lastly, I thank you. I'm honored that you took the time to read this book.

# ABOUT THE AUTHOR

"Ordinary to Extraordinary" is something Erik Seversen lives by. Born into an average, middle-class family in a suburb of Tacoma, Washington, Erik had unusually lofty goals, and he didn't listen when others said he was a dreamer. In fact, he turned those dreams into reality constructing a fulfilled life of success and adventure.

Erik studied anthropology at UCLA and the University of Virginia, and used anthropology in business, helping a company grow from $7 million to over $100 million in ten years doing international business development. He also taught English as a second language for ten years in Japan, France, Thailand, and at universities in the USA. Erik uses entrepreneurial success formulas and motivational materials in business, but he's also pioneering their use in the field of education.

Erik has traveled to over 80 countries around the world and 49 states in the USA. He has ridden a motorcycle on six continents and twice crossed the USA on one. He also climbs mountains and has summited the highest peaks of nine countries and eight states. Experiences ranging from discussing philosophy at cafés in Paris to having a machine gun stuck in his mouth in Nigeria to living with a remote

Indian tribe in the Amazon have forged in him a unique perspective that Erik uses to work through big life questions as well as small everyday decisions.

Erik is a writer, speaker, adventurer, entrepreneur, and educator who refuses to let others tell him what he can and cannot do. Erik's travels and intersections with people from around the world haven't been just a fun romp around the planet. They were a deep study of people, love, struggle, and ways of thinking that he relies on to tackle problems in school, business, and life.

Erik's most current ambitions are sharing the lessons he's learned with others and climbing mountains, which he says makes everyday challenges seem a lot easier.

Erik lives in Los Angeles with his wife and two boys.

# CONNECT WITH ERIK

Erik is on a mission to make people's lives more fulfilled. He helps people find purpose in their lives and success in their businesses. Ways you can work with Erik include English language coaching, motivational and practical business and entrepreneurship coaching, and life mindset coaching. He is a master at helping others go from knowledge to action.

Erik is also available for public speaking, seminars, and workshops.

Connect with Erik:

- Website: www.ErikSeversen.com
- Email: Erik@ErikSeversen.com

*THE EXTRAORDINARY HABITS CHALLENGE—Dare to Do It!*

The Extraordinary Habits Challenge *is a list of simple mental and physical habits that, when implemented into your routine, will greatly increase your energy, productivity, and sense of fulfillment. These habits will help you continue along the path of extraordinary success. Check it out right now at* www.ErikSeversen.com.